Silvester O'Fl

Come and See

LECTIO DIVINA WITH JOHN'S GOSPEL

the columba press

First published in 1999 by
the columba press
55A Spruce Avenue, Stillorgan Industrial Park, Blackrock, Co Dublin

Reprinted 1999

Cover by Bill Bolger
The cover picture is a detail from the portrait of John in the *Book of Kells* and is used by kind permission of the Board of Trinity College, Dublin.
Origination by The Columba Press
Printed in Ireland by Colour Books Ltd, Dublin

ISBN 1 85607 265 7

Acknowledgements
The bible texts are from *The Christian Community Bible* and are used by kind permission of Claretian Publications, Quezon City, Philippines.
The English translation of *The Catechism of the Catholic Church* is copyright (for Ireland) © 1994 Veritas Publications and Libreria Editrice Vaticana. All rights reserved.

Nihil Obstat:
Patrick Muldoon DD

Imprimatur:
✠ Philip Boyce
Bishop of Raphoe

Copyright © 1999, Silvester O'Flynn OFM Cap.

Contents

Foreword		5
John 1:1-18:	The Prologue	9
John 1:19-34:	John the Baptist	15
John 1:35-51:	The First Disciples	18
John 2:1-12:	The Wedding at Cana	23
John 2:13-25:	The New Temple	27
John 3:1-21:	Encounter with Nicodemus	31
John 4: 1-42:	The Samaritan Woman	39
John 4:43-54:	The Second Sign	46
John 5:1-47:	Healing on the Sabbath	50
John 6:1-71:	The Bread of Life	58
John 7 & 8:	Feast of Tabernacles	68
John 9:1-41:	Light for the Blind	81
John 10: 1-21:	The Good Shepherd	86
John 10:22-39:	The Feast of Dedication	91
John 10:40-11:44:	Raising of Lazarus	95
John 12: 1-50:	Lifted Up	102
John 13:	Before the Passover	108
John 14:	Motives for Consolation	114
John 15:	The True Vine	121
John 16:	Time after Jesus	126
John 17:	The Priestly Prayer of Jesus	132
John 18-19:	The Passing of Jesus	138
John 20:	The Empty Tomb	148
John 21:	Breakfast on the Shore	162
Signs of Faith		170
Mary at Cana and Calvary		174

Foreword

There are so many books already available on John's gospel, why another one? The sacred word of scripture is a seed that continues to sprout into new life like the fresh flowers of each spring. Scripture is a fountain that we drink from but never exhaust its wells. There never will be a time when all that can be said or written about the scriptures will be completed.

This book is an application of the process of *Lectio Divina* to John. *Lectio Divina* is a very old way of reading the scriptures which has returned to popularity today. It is a divine reading in the sense that one believes that the Spirit who first inspired the text is present in the soul of the believer who reads and prays with the text today.

In *Lectio Divina* one lovingly ponders on the scriptures to see what God did in the past so as to discern what God is doing in our lives today. Familiarity with God's past deeds enables one to recognise where God is today.

The process of *Lectio Divina* involves three steps, *lectio*, *meditatio* and *oratio*. Then it leads to the fruit of *contemplatio*.

Lectio – one reads the text, not just once but several times. One absorbs the words and phrases and lets them soak into memory and imagination. To get a better understanding of what it means, a commentary may be helpful. In the short commentary that I offer with each episode I pay special attention to John's symbolic use of numbers and to the context of Jewish feasts which open up the fuller meaning of events.

Meditatio – one makes the connection between the text of the past and life today. The classical example of this connecting occurred on the day that Jesus returned to the synagogue in

Nazareth. He read from the Prophet Isaiah. Then he rolled up the scroll, handed it to the attendant and said: 'Today these prophetic words come true even as you listen' (Lk 4:21). Jesus moved from what Isaiah had said in the past to what the Spirit was about to do in his mission of good news.

In this book I follow the commentary with a section called *Connecting*. Obviously there is no counting the directions one might go with any text. Hopefully, the connections I make will encourage readers to explore their own train of thought arising out of the sacred words. I make extensive use of *The Catechism of the Catholic Church* as I find in it the wisdom of the Holy Spirit clearly guiding the church of today in bringing to mind all that is contained in the words and deeds of Jesus.

Oratio – one is moved to pray to God whose presence in our life today is discerned in the light of the scripture. The disciples on the road to Emmaus felt their hearts burning within them as the risen Lord applied the scriptures to what they had experienced in Jerusalem. In prayer, the heart expands in expressions of adoration, love, thanksgiving, asking and repentance. Prayer which grows from pondering the scriptures will be full of biblical imagery and phrases. The prayer that I add to each episode is by way of example and encouragement to readers to develop their own sighs of the heart. Each prayer is expressed in the first person plural for the benefit of groups who will use this book.

The regular practice of *Lectio Divina* develops an attitude of contemplation. The word *contemplation* has its roots in a Greek word associated with measuring. Temperature is the measurement of heat, temperament describes character. A template is a flat design cut to a required shape to guide a tradesman's knife or scissors. The original pagan temple was a sacred area measured by the movements of the lights in the sky. A contemplative life is one that is measured by the heavenly light of divine revelation. This is the fruit of living each day with mind and heart attuned to God through familiarity with the word of God.

The gospel according to John has been compared to a marvellous swimming pool in which the infant can paddle and the elephant can swim. For those who get in at the shallow end it contains some very appealing stories, like the meeting of Jesus with the woman at the well. One will also be delighted with the many wonderful sayings like, *Come and see ... Peace I leave you ... I am the way, the truth and the life ... I am the Good Shepherd ... The Word was made flesh and lived among us.*

When one ventures in at the deep end, there are depths of meaning to be explored. John leads the reader from everyday matters like water, wine, bread or sickness to the heights of divine revelation in God's invitation to us to share in divine life.

John has traditionally been depicted as the eagle, the bird that soars aloft on mighty wings. Furthermore, the eagle is reputed to be the only creature that can look directly into the light of the sun without damaging its eyes. John is the writer who looks into the light of divine life, revealing more about the relationships of the Father, the Son and the Holy Spirit than any other writer. For John, Jesus is the Word made flesh, the revelation of the Father.

No one has ever seen God
but the only Son made him known:
the one who is in and with the Father (Jn 1:19).

As Jesus replied to Philip: 'Whoever sees me sees the Father: how can you say: "Show us the Father?" Do you not believe that I am in the Father and the Father is in me?' (Jn 14: 9-10).

> Jesus said, 'Come and see.'
> So they saw where he stayed
> and spent the rest of that day with him (Jn 1:39).

John 1:1-18: The Prologue

¹In the beginning was the Word
And the Word was with God
and the Word was God;
²he was in the beginning with God.

³All things were made through him
and without him nothing came to be.
⁴Whatever has come to be, found life in him,
life which for humans was also light.
⁵Light that shines in the dark;
light that darkness could not overcome.

⁶A man came, sent by God;
his name was John.
⁷He came to bear witness,
as a witness to introduce the Light
so that all might believe through him.
⁸He was not the Light
but a witness to introduce the Light.

⁹For the Light was coming into the world,
the true Light that enlightens everyone.
¹⁰He was already in the world
and through him the world was made,
the very world that did not know him.
¹¹He came to his own,
yet his own people did not receive him;
¹²but all who have received him
he empowers to become children of God
for they believe in his Name.
¹³This birth is without seed
or carnal desire or will of man:
they are born of God.

¹⁴And the Word was made flesh
and dwelt among us;
and we have seen his Glory,
the Glory of the only Son
coming from the Father:
fulness of truth and loving-kindness.

¹⁵John bore witness to him openly, saying:
This is the one who comes after me
but he is already ahead of me
for he was before me.

¹⁶From his fullness we have all received,
favour upon favour.
¹⁷For God had given us the Law through Moses,
but Loving-kindness and Faithfulness
came through Jesus Christ.
¹⁸No one has ever seen God,
but the only Son made him known:
the one who is in and with the Father.

Every book has a background. No child ever came to birth without parents who generated and carried it from conception to birth. Similarly, every book is a child of earlier books, inheriting their thoughts, imagery and style, but now given a new existence. The gospels were no exception.

Matthew, Mark and Luke portrayed Jesus in the light of what the prophets had written, especially about the Suffering Servant of God, an innocent victim on behalf of others. However, John's predecessors were the Wisdom books. He does not trace the human genealogy of Jesus but develops his divine origin through use of the Greek concept of *Logos,* translated as the Word. This emphasises how there is thought before action, a plan before production. The Old Testament Wisdom literature had prepared for John in its familiarity with Greek thought. 'With you is Wisdom that knows your works, that was present when you made the world and is aware of what is pleasing in your eyes and what is right according to your commandments' (Wis 9:9).

JOHN 1:1-18: PROLOGUE

In the Prologue to the gospel John sketches the vast timescale of God's action from the eons before creation down to the coming of Jesus in human flesh. Jesus is introduced as the Word of God. John develops the coming of the Word in five stages.

1. Jesus is the eternal Word
In the inner depths of the Sacred Trinity, the Father expresses total fullness in the Son. In the perfection of divine expression one Word says all.

> In the beginning was the Word
> And the Word was with God
> And the Word was God;
> he was in the beginning with God.

Jesus is eternal in terms of time since he is before all ages.

And he is eternal in terms of fullness of grace and truth, being the perfect expression of the Father.

2. Jesus is the creating Word
He is the Word through whom all things are created. In the bible's first account of creation, God did not so much make things as say things into life.

> God said, 'Let there be light'; and there was light (Gen 1:3).

The word of God creates life.

> All things were made through him
> and without him nothing came to be (1:3).

Everything in creation is sacred since it originated in God's spoken Word. The sensitive soul is aware of God in all the wonders of creation, great and small. There are 'tongues in trees, books in the running brooks, sermons in stones, and good in everything' (Shakespeare). Saint Paul said that the everlasting power of God is there for people to see in all created things (Rom 1:20). The great mystic, Francis of Assisi, saw the hand of the divine artist in all the artistry of nature.

3. Jesus is the revealing Word
He is the Word of light
> For the Light was coming into the world,
> the true Light that enlightens everyone (1:9).

There are religions which are based on the mysteries of the natural world. Others that follow the writings of great sages. The Jewish-Christian tradition is based on the belief that God made direct revelation to human beings. Revelation began with Abraham and reached its climax in the coming of Jesus Christ. John the Baptist was the last of the prophets preparing the way for Jesus. The Baptist's role is that of a witness.

He was not the Light but a witness to introduce the Light (1:8). Jesus, the Word of God, was the true light that gives light to all people.

4. Jesus is the Word in human flesh
He came down from heaven and dwelt amongst us. What John says in Greek is that he pitched his tent amongst us. He did not set up a permanent home to stay forever in human form. His presence was for the temporary span of human life, from birth to death.

John writes with the deep conviction of an eyewitness. 'We have seen his glory.' We can say that, in Jesus, God is speaking to us in the language of a human life. This is the familiar language of everyday life. If we want to know more about God, the surest way is to study Jesus every day.

The writer, John, is the eagle who looks straight into the light of the sun. John sees the glory of God filtered to the limitations of our eyes through the humanity of Jesus. In his humanity, the grace of God and the truth of God were revealed to us.

5. Jesus is the inviting Word
Jesus respected people's freedom. He did not force himself on them. His life was an invitation to people to respond to his way, his truth and the life he was offering.

As we go through this gospel, we will see that everything Jesus did or said drew a reaction from people. Some rejected him, others accepted. The sad verse says that 'He came to his

JOHN 1:1-18: PROLOGUE

own yet his own people did not accept him' (1:11). The happy response is that others did accept him. And what happened? He gave them power to become children of God.

The key to accepting Jesus is faith. It is important to recognise that faith is more than a one-day act of commitment. It is an on-going response over months and into years. The life of grace grows and deepens, grace upon grace, favour upon favour. The more one has grown in faith, the more one can receive of grace and truth. That is how memory works for us too. The more the mind knows, the greater the number of connecting points for the mind to attach new facts. The more we co-operate with God's favours, the better we are able to receive more grace.

Connecting

We have identified five stages in the coming of Jesus – the Word from all eternity, in creation, in revelation, in human flesh and inviting. We find these five stages echoed in the *Catechism of the Catholic Church*, 142.

> By his revelation, the invisible God from the fullness of his love addresses people as his friends, and moves among them, in order to invite and receive them into his own company. The adequate response to this invitation is faith.

Every episode in this gospel will show how people rejected or accepted the invitation of God. To those who did accept Jesus, God gave the gift of divine adoption in the power to become children of God. The work of God creating, revealing and inviting continues in our lives. There are questions that each one must answer personally.

Do you have a reverence for all created things as coming from the creative word of God?

In your faith how do you experience God coming to you?

In what ways do you experience God as your light?

Are you sensitive to the ways in which God invites you?

How aware are you of accepting or rejecting God's coming every day?

Does the awesome privilege of sharing in divine life mean much to you?

Praying

O Jesus, you are the sacred Word of the Father, God from God, light from light, true God from true God, begotten not made.

Through you all things were made. Open up our sensitivity to see your presence in all of creation. May our hearts expand in wonder and praise.

In the fullness of time you came into our world. You lived among us. You humbled yourself to share in our humanity so that we might be lifted up to share in your divinity.

Since we share in your divine life, we dare to call God *Our Father*. You invite us to participate, though sacred liturgy, in your eternal return of worship to the Father. May grace grow upon grace as we appreciate the awesome privilege that is ours in sacred liturgy.

The Word was made flesh and lived among us. May our daily Angelus be a faith-filled celebration of the wonders of your incarnation.

John 1:19-34: John the Baptist

¹⁹This was the testimony of John when the Jews sent priests and Levites to ask him, 'Who are you?' ²⁰John recognized the truth and did not deny it. He said, 'I am not the Messiah.' ²¹And they asked him, 'Then, who are you? Elijah?' He answered, 'I am not.' They said, 'Are you the Prophet?' And he answered, 'No.' ²²Then they said to him, 'Tell us who you are, so that we can give some answer to those who sent us. How do you see yourself?' ²³And John said, quoting the prophet Isaiah, 'I am the voice crying out in the wilderness: Make straight the way of the Lord.' ²⁴These persons had been sent by the Pharisees; ²⁵so they put a further question to John: 'Then, why are you baptizing if you are not the Messiah, or Elijah, or the Prophet?' ²⁶John answered, 'I baptize you with water but among you stands one whom you do not know; ²⁷although he comes after me, I am not worthy to untie the strap of his sandal.'
²⁸This happened in Bethany beyond the Jordan, where John was baptising.
²⁹The next day John saw Jesus coming towards him and said, 'There is the Lamb of God, who takes away the sin of the world. ³⁰It is he of whom I said: A man comes after me who is already ahead of me, for he was before me. ³¹I myself did not know him, but I came baptising to prepare for him, so that he might be revealed in Israel.'
³²And John also gave this testimony, 'I saw the Spirit coming down on him like a dove from heaven and resting on him. ³³I myself did not know him but God who sent me to baptise told me: 'You will see the Spirit coming down and resting on the one who baptizes with the Holy Spirit.' ³⁴Yes, I have seen! and I declare that this is the Chosen One of God.'

In this gospel, any time John the Baptist is mentioned it is emphasised that his task was to prepare the way for Jesus and to hand over to him. It seems that when the gospel was being written there still existed pockets of followers of the Baptist who had not advanced to belief in Jesus. Hence the writer's emphasis on the witnessing role of the Baptist.

Three times we hear the Baptist say 'I am not ...' By contrast, this gospel contains seven great I am statements of Jesus.

'I am not the Christ.' He does not claim to be the Messiah.

'I am not Elijah.' Many people expected that Elijah, who had been taken off to heaven in a fiery chariot, would come to prepare for the Messiah.

'I am not the Prophet.' This refers to Deuteronomy 18:15 where God promises to raise up a prophet like Moses from among the brothers. As we go through the gospel we will find other references to this expected prophet.

When pressed to say who he is, the Baptist quotes Isaiah: 'I am the voice crying out in the wilderness: Make straight the way of the Lord.'

John is the voice. Jesus is the Word. The voice is there to serve the word. John prepares the way. Jesus is the way.

John led people to express their repentance by washing in water. Jesus would lead them beyond the washing to receiving the Holy Spirit.

Later on, towards the end of Chapter 3, John the Baptist describes himself as the bridegroom's friend (the best man) who is happy to hand over to the groom. 'It is necessary that he increase but that I decrease.'

Connecting

The calendar of the liturgical year beautifully counterpoints the declining light of the Baptist with the increasing light of Christ. The birthday of the Baptist is celebrated on June twenty-fourth, mid-summer, when the sun begins to wane. The birth of Christ is celebrated around mid-winter, when the light of the sun begins to increase.

The humble self-effacement of the Baptist offers a very relevant challenge to today's brash culture which encourages unlimited self-fulfilment. It is a mark of wisdom to achieve the correct balance between the opposite sides of life.

There is a time to develop our talents and to thank God for the wonder of our being.

But there is also a time to stop pushing ourselves forward and to step back from the limelight. Otherwise we tend to make little gods of ourselves. Selfishness finds comfortable respectability under psychological jargon. Too much emphasis on self-fulfilment has drawn people away from the gospel spirit of denying self in order to find the fullness of life.

John the Baptist was enthusiastic about his ministry. But he was happy to stand back from the limelight once Jesus came along.

Praying

Lord, help us to learn from the humility of John the Baptist.

May we live in the truth so that we humbly acknowledge what we are not. Help us to let go of the false masks of all that we pretend to be.

May it be our joy, as it was John's, to recognise you as the source of the Holy Spirit for our lives.

May it be our peace to know you as the one who takes away the sins of the world.

May it be our desire to serve you, to be a voice to your word, a witness to your way.

You alone lead us out of the wilderness.

Not to us, O Lord, not to us but to your name be the glory.

John 1:35-51: The First Disciples

[35]On the following day John was standing there again with two of his disciples. [36]As Jesus walked by, John looked at him and said, 'There is the Lamb of God.' [37]On hearing this, the two disciples followed Jesus. [38]He turned and saw them following, and he said to them, 'What are you looking for?' They answered, 'Rabbi (which means Master), where are you staying?' [39]Jesus said, 'Come and see.' So they went and saw where he stayed and spent the rest of that day with him. It was about four o'clock in the afternoon.
[40]Andrew, the brother of Simon Peter, was one of the two who heard what John had said and followed Jesus. [41]Early the next morning he found his brother Simon and said to him, 'We have found the Messiah' (which means the Christ), [42]and he brought Simon to Jesus. Jesus looked at him and said, 'You are Simon, son of John, but you shall be called Cephas' (which means Rock).
[43]The next day, Jesus decided to set off for Galilee. He found Philip and said to him, 'Follow me.' [44]Philip was from Bethsaida, the town of Andrew and Peter. [45]Philip found Nathanael and said to him, 'We have found the one that Moses wrote about in the Law, and the prophets as well: he is Jesus, son of Joseph, from Nazareth.'
[46]Nathanael replied, 'Can anything good come from Nazareth?' Philip said to him, 'Come and see.' [47]When Jesus saw Nathanael coming, he said of him, 'Here comes an Israelite, a true one; there is nothing false in him.' [48]Nathanael asked him, 'How do you know me?' And Jesus said to him, 'Before Philip called you, you were under the fig tree and I saw you.'
[49]Nathanael answered, 'Master you are the Son of God! You are the King of Israel!' [50]But Jesus replied, 'You believe because I said: "I saw you under the fig tree." But you will see greater things than that.
[51]Truly, I say to you, you will see the heavens opened and the angels of God ascending and descending upon the Son of Man.'

JOHN 1:35-51: THE FIRST DISCIPLES

Was the evangelist, John, a reporter who recorded events as they happened, or a reflective writer who made a creative use of the facts to bring out their wider significance and deeper meaning? Obviously John was the second kind of writer.

His account of the first contact of Jesus with his close disciples takes liberties with time. The gradual growth of the disciples in their understanding of Jesus is bypassed. So we see Simon getting his new name, Peter, at this first encounter with Jesus. Jesus is called by various titles which were recognised much later according to the synoptics. The synoptics were much closer to the historical development.

John takes this liberty with time because his whole gospel is written in the light of the risen Lord to whom yesterday, today and tomorrow are an eternal present. As John is in a hurry to get into the depths of the story, he uses this first encounter of Jesus with the disciples to condense many of the insights of Paul and the synoptics. He brings forward various disciples who refer to Jesus by names which would not have been used until a much later understanding of Jesus and his ministry.

John the Baptist calls Jesus the Lamb of God. This one title condenses much of the theology of St Paul regarding Jesus as the new Passover Lamb whose sacrificial death-resurrection was the great act of justification before the Father, replacing obedience to the Law as the means of justification.

Next in line are two disciples of the Baptist, one of whom we are later told is Andrew. They call Jesus 'Rabbi' meaning teacher. As yet Jesus had not begun his teaching ministry. But the evangelist, John, uses the title of teacher on the presumption that that the reader is familiar with the teaching of Jesus from the other three gospels, the synoptics.

Early next day Andrew refers to Jesus as the Messiah, the Christ. We know from Mark and Matthew that it took a considerable time before any disciple called Jesus the Christ. Again, John is contracting the time of development by condensing what the synoptics had written.

Then Philip identifies Jesus as the one that Moses and the

prophets wrote about. This is a neat way of summing up the books that we know as the Old Testament.

Finally, Nathanael calls Jesus the Son of God and the King of Israel. In these titles we are given the highest insights of the synoptics.

Thus by foreshortening what was really a gradual growth in the understanding of Jesus, it is as if John were telling the reader that we are going to take Paul and the other gospels as read. So now, read on because we have so much more to learn about Jesus. 'Truly, I say to you, you will see the heavens opened and the angels of God ascending and descending upon the Son of Man' (1:51).

Nathanael, the true Israelite
What did Jesus mean by telling Nathanael that he saw him under the fig tree? The simplest explanation is that the broadleafed fig tree afforded a perfect shade for outdoor teaching and, there, Jesus had observed Nathanael teaching.

'Can anything good come from Nazareth?'

Some scholars point out that the name Nazareth comes from the Hebrew word for a branch. If a play on the name is intended then we must hear Jesus asking, 'Can anything good come from Branch?'

Anyone familiar with the Old Testament would recall promises about the branch of Juda (Gen 49:10), the branch of Jesse (Is 11:1) and the branch of David's line (Jer 23:3). A very significant passage in Zech 3:8-10 links a promised Branch with sitting under the fig tree. 'Listen further, O high priest Joshua ... I am going to bring my servant the Branch ... On that day, you will invite one another under your vines and fig trees.' Jesus, then, was saying that the Branch of Nazareth had borne fruit and that Nathanael and others were invited now to partake of a teaching greater than anything heard before.

Nathanael was called a true Israelite, a man with no guile or deceit. This is interesting. The Israelites were descendants of Israel, whose original name was Jacob. This Jacob was quite a trickster, anything but a man without guile. He had even deceived his blind father, Isaac, to obtain the blessing due to his brother Esau. The change in Jacob came when he wrestled with an angel. He was wounded in the contest and left with a limp but he held on until he was rewarded with a blessing. Then he received the new name, Israel, which means the strength of God (Gen 32:23-30). The link with Jacob is strengthened as Jesus calls to mind the dream of Jacob in which he saw a ladder linking heaven and earth with the angels ascending and descending (Gen 28:10ff.).

Nathanael, representing the true descendants of Israel, is being told that the dreams and prophecies of the past were about to be fulfilled in the flowering of the Branch of Nazareth.

Connecting

The encounter of Jesus with the first disciples is an event about searching, invitation and promise.

Searching

In the story there are constant references to looking and seeing. We read of the searching by various disciples and of the penetrating look of Jesus into the innermost heart. The Baptist looked in wonder at Jesus before identifying him as the Lamb of God.

Jesus looked intently at Simon, penetrating to the inmost heart of the man he would call Cephas (Aramaic) or Peter (Greek), the rock of the church.

Jesus saw Nathanael under the fig tree. Again, his eyes gazed at the pure heart of that good teacher. And the story leads to the prospect of seeing greater wonders.

We reflect on how the eye of God searches our innermost thoughts and sees our deepest motives. Yet this look is full of love and invites us to look towards Jesus. We hear him say: 'Come and see.'

Religions which do not have the revealed word of God are described as people's search for God. But the Jewish-Christian tradition is about God's search for his people. Jesus is that Good Shepherd who searches for the lost to invite them home.

Invitation
The words of the Lord in the story invite us to sit under the branch.
'Come and see.'
'Follow me.'
'They went and saw where he lived and spent the rest of the day with him.' John notes that it was about the tenth hour, four in the afternoon. It suggests that the day's journey is over. The searching soul has found home with the Lord. What is important thereafter is to spend time with the Lord.

Promise
With the Lord there is no end to the possibilities of relationship which are opened up. The recall of Jacob's dream about the angels moving between heaven and earth represents a dynamic relationship between God and humanity. His promise opens up expectations for the rest of the gospel.

John has summarised the promises of the Old Testament and the insights of Paul and the synoptics as he whets our appetites for the greater story he is to reveal.

Praying
'Come and see ... follow me.' Lord Jesus, we hear your words of invitation addressed to us personally. Grant us the grace to know you in prayer. May we experience prayer as a time when we look at you as you are looking at us ... lovers, enjoying your presence, happy to spend time with you.

We pray for those who do not know you. Break through the clouds that darken their lives. Let the light of your face smile upon them and draw them to follow you.

Let the heavens open up and may your holy angels lift up our prayers to you and draw down your protection on us.

O Lord, prepare our hearts for all the wonders that you have in store for us ... greater things than anything seen yet ... greater beyond our highest dreams.

John 2:1-12: The Wedding at Cana

[1]Three days later there was a wedding at Cana in Galilee and the mother of Jesus was there. [2]Jesus was also invited to the wedding with his disciples. [3]When all the wine provided for the celebration had been served and they had run out of wine the mother of Jesus said to him, 'They have no wine.' [4]Jesus replied, 'Woman, your thoughts are not mine! My hour has not yet come.'
[5]However his mother said to the servants, 'Do whatever he tells you.'
[6]Nearby were six stone water jars meant for the ritual washing as practised by the Jews; each jar could hold twenty or thirty gallons.
[7]Jesus said to the servants, 'Fill the jars with water.' And they filled them to the brim.
[8]Then Jesus said, 'Now draw some out and take it to the steward.' So they did.
[9]The steward tasted the water that had become wine, without knowing from where it had come; for only the servants who had drawn the water knew. So, he immediately called the bridegroom [10]to tell him, 'Everyone serves the best wine first and when people have drunk enough, he serves that which is ordinary. You instead have kept the best wine until the end.'
[11]This miraculous sign was the first, and Jesus performed it at Cana in Galilee. In this way he let his Glory appear and his disciples believed in him.
[12]After this, Jesus went down to Capernaum with his mother, his brothers and his disciples; and they stayed there for a few days.

There was a wedding at Cana in Galilee. The names of bride and groom are not mentioned because the wedding which interests John is the joining of heaven and earth. Already the greater things promised to Nathanael are being manifested. Heaven is opened and not merely angels, but the Son of God has come down to lift up his chosen bride.

The amount of new wine is enormous, eight hundred bottles or more in modern measurement. John clearly wants the reader to treat this story on more than a literal level.

A major motif in this gospel is the way that Jesus brought about the replacement of many time-honoured Jewish feasts and institutions. At Cana, in this wedding of heaven and earth, the old religion which was represented by the water for ritual purification is changed into the new religion which is characterised by the wine of celebration.

It was the third day, and in the world of story this is usually when things happen. But it was also the seventh day, if one were to count the days since that first encounter with the Baptist. The third and seventh days were the days for ritual washing for the purification of defilement (Num 19:11). Notice that these jars were reserved for the water of purification and they were of stone to ensure cleanliness. The jars numbered six, still short of the sacredness of seven.

The mother of Jesus was there. John, in his gospel, never mentions Mary by name. We will notice as we go through the gospel that he sometimes refrains from giving us the name of somebody, probably because he wants us to consider that person not only as an individual but as a representative of others. The mother of Jesus is a title that refers not only to Mary but to the stock of Israel, the racial mother of Jesus.

'They have no wine,' says this representative of Mother Israel. 'My people have a religion of laws, of purification and water. But they have lost the sense of a loving God, a God of wine and celebration.'

It is significant, then, that it was the water reserved for purification which was changed into wine. Brimming over, an extravagant celebration of God's unstinted giving. The best wine was produced to celebrate the wedding of God and humanity.

The fact that Jesus used the ministry of servants, literally deacons, and the water to provide the wine hints at the principle of the later sacraments. God chooses to work through the sacred use of human actions and material elements.

John tells us that this was the first of the signs through which Jesus let his glory appear. John treats the miracles of Jesus as signs. Signs get their importance from what they indicate. The miracles of Jesus were signs which pointed to his divinity which, in itself, could not be seen directly. The miraculous signs of Jesus drew people to believing in him. After the first sign, the disciples learned to believe.

The role of Mary in this story is very important but we shall leave it aside until a later development when we can link it up with her presence on Calvary.

Connecting

Our God, as revealed at Cana, passionately longs to embrace us in divine union.

We meet many joyless people who live in constant fear of a stern, joyless God. Their religion is dominated by guilt and punishment. They are still at the stage of washing and do not appreciate the brimming wine of celebration. There is a point worth noting about Christian sects. The name *sect* indicates a group who have a section of the Christian heritage. The vast majority of sects do not have the Eucharist and they constantly harp on being saved or on the need for legal justification from the defilement of sin. It seems that they are back in the days of ritual ablution. They have the water of baptism but they have no wine. Significantly, neither do they fully appreciate the role of Mary in the plan of salvation.

We also meet people whose God is aloof and distant. They accept the existence of a Supreme Being but they do not enjoy any sort of meaningful, personal relationship with God. There are people who go through the motions of religious ceremony but fight shy of intimacy with God.

At Cana, God is shown as reaching out to us. The time of courtship is over. God, come down to us in Jesus, embraces straying humankind and draws us into a life of union. God came down to us in order to lift us up.

This God reaches out to us in a daily sharing of life, light and love. The Creator God shares life with us. Even the simplest action, like blinking an eyelid or lifting my little finger, is done with an energy given me by the Creator.

The Word of God has brought divine light to us. To believe in Jesus is to walk in his light. It is a way of life that leads away from sin and the utter darkness of despair.

And the love of God is given to us principally in the gift of the Holy Spirit.

At Cana, God encounters the world as a loving, embracing and celebrating God who wants us to give up our hearts to divine union.

Is this your idea of God?

Is this the heart of your faith and religion?

Praying

O God of abundant giving, the enormous amount of new wine is an indication of your store of blessings.

O God of the wedding, you reach down to us to take us to yourself in intimate love. As you let your glory be seen and the disciples believed in you, may we not lack abundant signs of your love, nor the eyes to see them. We pray for those who do not believe: that their eyes will be opened to see the signs of your presence and power in the world: that they will be drawn into the embrace of your love.

Lord, as you showed your power and divinity at a wedding, we pray for all married couples. Strengthen the bonds of those who are drifting apart. Help all families to grow in the likeness of your love. Take the water of our human efforts and transform it into the wine of divine love.

John 2:13-25: The New Temple

[13] As the Passover of the Jews was at hand, Jesus went up to Jerusalem. [14] In the Temple court he found merchants selling oxen, sheep and doves, and money-changers seated at their tables. [15] Making a whip of cords, he drove them all out of the Temple court, together with the oxen and sheep. He knocked over the tables of the money-changers, scattering the coins, [16] and ordered the people selling doves, 'Take all this away and stop turning my Father's house into a marketplace!'
[17] His disciples recalled the words of Scripture: Zeal for your House devours me as a fire.
[18] The Jews then questioned Jesus, 'Where are the miraculous signs which give you the right to do this?' [19] And Jesus said, 'Destroy this temple and in three days I will raise it up.'
[20] The Jews then replied, 'The building of this temple has already taken forty-six years, and you will raise it up in three days?'
[21] Actually, Jesus was referring to the temple of his body. [22] Only when he had risen from the dead did his disciples remember these words; then they believed both the Scripture and the words Jesus had spoken.
[23] Jesus stayed in Jerusalem during the Passover Festival and many believed in his Name when they saw the miraculous signs he performed. [24] But Jesus did not trust himself to them, because he knew all of them. [25] He didn't need any evidence about anyone for he himself knew what there is in man.

At the wedding feast at Cana, Jesus had indicated the advance from a religion of washing to a religion of celebrating union with God. The next expression of the new religion is the replacement of the temple of stone by the temple of the risen Lord.

The temple was the sacred house of God. The Jews believed that the one God is everywhere and that people could meet God in prayer at any place or time. God did not need a house made by human hands. It was the people who needed the building as a suitable place of assembly for celebrating the great feasts.

Before the Passover
The time-setting is important. It was before the Jewish Passover. Two other Passover feasts will occur in this gospel: one associated with Jesus as the bread of life; the other being the time of his return to the Father.

Preparation for the Passover involved a thorough searching of each house to cleanse it of the slightest crumb of unleavened food. In this context Jesus cleansed the House of God of all that had defiled it by turning the house of prayer into a huckster's market. The cleansing of the temple is one of the few incidents recorded by all four evangelists but each one drew a different lesson from it. In John's gospel the action of Jesus is a judgement of God on the temple and on Jewish institutions.

Reactions to Jesus
People reacted to the claims of Jesus in different ways: some were moved to believe in him; others hardened in their rejection. It was by remembering the words of scripture that the disciples found faith: 'Zeal for your house devours me like a fire.'

Those who rejected Jesus are called the Jews. While it is true that Jesus and his disciples were also Jews, John's use of the term expresses the situation at his time of writing. By then the Christian community was clearly separated from the Jews.

Instead of accepting Jesus in faith, these Jews intervened and questioned Jesus, not in questions seeking light but in an aggressive, accusing manner. They demand a sign of Jesus to justify what he has done.

The answer of Jesus is enigmatic. 'Destroy this temple and in three days I will raise it up.' The temple he spoke about was the sanctuary of God's presence which was his body. But the Jews remain on the material level, talking about the temple of stone which had taken forty-six years to build. The disciples, however, in the time of resurrection remembered his words and they believed the words of scripture.

Connecting

Everything in John's gospel is written in the light of the resurrection. The significance of the cleansing of the temple was appreciated by the disciples only after the rising of Jesus from the dead. They understood then that the great meeting place with God would no longer be identified with a temple in Jerusalem but in and through the risen Lord Jesus. In him alone is true access to the Father.

At Passover time the temple was the location for the sacrifice of many animals. At the third Passover in this gospel Jesus will be identified as the Lamb of God whose death is sacrificial. The essence of sacrifice, *sacrum-facere*, is in the giving or going to the Holy One. All previous sacrifices found their completion in the dying and rising of Jesus. His going from this world to the Father is the perfect sacrifice.

It is the holy privilege of Christians to participate in this perfect sacrifice in the celebration of the Eucharist. There, united with the risen Lord, we pray: 'Through him, with him and in him, in the unity of the Holy Spirit, all glory and honour is yours, almighty Father, for ever and ever.'

The risen Lord is the new temple. St Paul so understood the union of the baptised with Christ that he extends the title temple to Christians too, both in the collective sense of the Christian community and in the individual sense of the sanctified body of the baptised. In the ceremony of baptism, immediately after the pouring of water (or immersion), the newly baptised is anointed with the oil of chrism. This signifies one's union with Christ as prophet, priest and king. The celebrant prays: 'So may you live always as a member of his body, sharing everlasting life.'

St Paul appeals to this idea of our bodies being temples of the Holy Spirit to encourage the Corinthians to keep themselves free from sexual immorality. 'Did you not know that your body is a temple of the Holy Spirit within you, given by God? You belong no longer to yourselves. Remember at what price you have been bought and make your body serve the glory of God' (1 Cor 6:19-20).

Praying

O Jesus, in the years of your life on earth you were the holy temple of God's presence among people. Now, in the age of resurrection, you raise up all who believe in you to take their place in the temple of true worship of the Father ... in you, through you and with you ... by the power of your Holy Spirit.

You know what resides in the inner heart of every person. Grant us your grace to cleanse our minds, hearts and bodies of all defilement and attachment to sin.

As the psalmist was devoured by love and zeal for your house, so may the Holy Spirit set our hearts on fire with enthusiasm for the sacred life that you have shared with us in baptism.

And so, Lord Jesus, with our bodies cleansed of sin and our hearts aflame with your love, may we take our place in your temple of glory and honour to the Father.

John 3:1-21 Encounter with Nicodemus

¹Among the Pharisees there was a ruler of the Jews named Nicodemus. ²He came to Jesus at night and said, 'Rabbi, we know that you have come from God to teach us, for no one can perform miraculous signs like yours unless God is with him.'
³Jesus replied, 'Truly, I say to you, no one can see the kingdom of God unless he is born again from above.'
⁴Nicodemus said, 'How can there be rebirth for a grown man? Who could go back to his mother's womb and be born again?' ⁵Jesus replied, 'Truly, I say to you: Unless one is born again of water and the Spirit, he cannot enter the kingdom of God. ⁶What is born of the flesh is flesh, and what is born of the Spirit is spirit. ⁷Because of this, don't be surprised when I say: 'You must be born again from above.'
⁸The wind blows where it pleases and you hear its sound, but you don't know where it comes from or where it is going. It is like that with everyone who is born of the Spirit.'
⁹Nicodemus asked again, 'How can this be?' ¹⁰And Jesus answered, 'You are a teacher in Israel, and yet you don't know these things!
¹¹Truly, I say to you, we speak of what we know and we tell about the things we have seen, but you don't accept our testimony. ¹²If you don't believe when I tell you earthly things what then, when I tell you heavenly things? ¹³Yet no one has ever gone up to heaven except the one who came from heaven, the Son of Man.
¹⁴As Moses lifted up the serpent in the desert, so must the Son of Man be lifted up, ¹⁵so that whoever believes in him may have eternal life.

At the end of the last chapter we were told that Jesus, who knew what was in human nature, did not trust himself to those who said that they believed. Nicodemus came along, believing that Jesus is a teacher sent by God. Yet the evangelist notes that he came at night, thereby indicating that Nicodemus was still in darkness. The encounter of Jesus with this leading Jewish teacher is the occasion for the third replacement of a Jewish institution.

First, the water of purification was changed into wine to celebrate the wedding of heaven and earth.

Next, the temple and its sacrifices would be replaced by a liturgy in and through the risen Jesus.

Now Nicodemus hears the news that his Jewish birth and teaching will not be sufficient for seeing the new kingdom of God. Natural human life needs to be lifted up to a supernatural level. This effectively involves a new birth or a birth from above (the Greek of John can be translated in either sense).

Nicodemus asks whether this new birth means that a person must re-enter the mother's womb. But Jesus explains that this is something different from birth in the flesh. 'What is born of the flesh is flesh, and what is born of the Spirit is spirit' (3:6). He then takes up the word *spirit* in the sense of the wind. The wind cannot be seen by the physical eye, yet its movements can be observed in the slanting of the smoke, the scurrying of the clouds or the race of ripples across water. In the same way, the invisible Spirit can be seen to be present through exterior works.

This new, supernatural birth occurs:
by the grace of the Holy Spirit:
which is voluntarily accepted:
and ritually expressed in the water of baptism.

Again, Nicodemus has a question. How can this be possible? Jesus explains that this lifting up of human nature is now possible because he has come down from heaven in order to lift us up. To illustrate the point he refers back to that strange incident in the Book of Numbers (21:4-9) at the time of Moses. The people were attacked by deadly, fiery serpents. God told Moses to fashion a serpent of bronze and hold it up on a standard before the people. All who had been bitten were to look up at the bronze serpent to be healed.

John's readers would recognise that Jesus was anticipating his own being lifted up on the cross and in resurrection. All who look up at the risen Lord with faith have the beginning of eternal life here and now. They are saved from the fatal sting of sin.

Connecting

Recently I met a young married couple who were trying to come to terms with the death of their young child. They were visited at home by two so-called evangelicals who told them that they would never see their child in heaven unless they were born again and come to know the Lord.

The line about the need to be born again (Jn 3:7) is frequently taken out of context and presented as the only absolute condition for salvation. We had a Spiritual Director in our student days who advised us to beware of the man of the one book!

The context of this encounter with Nicodemus is where the evangelist is showing how Jesus replaced various Jewish institutions and traditions. After transforming the purificatory water and the nature of the temple, the dialogue with Nicodemus is about the need for something more than birth into the Jewish heritage and faith. Nicodemus is presented as a leading Jew and a teacher in Israel. This encounter makes the point that birth into what this leading teacher represents is not sufficient. There must be a new beginning of life through faith in Jesus, celebrated in baptism. But what does this faith involve?

The Catechism of the Catholic Church teaches: 'By faith a person completely submits one's intellect and will to God. With one's whole being a person gives assent to God the revealer. Sacred Scripture calls this human response to God, the author of revelation, "the obedience of faith"' (CCC 143).

> The believer is one who says a resounding *yes* to God
> in the intellect which gives assent to divine teaching,
> in the will which desires to love and serve God,
> and in the practical actions of the whole of life since faith without good works is dead (Jas 1:16).

If we may speak in broad generalisations, Catholics tend to emphasise more the intellectual content of faith, testing the orthodoxy of doctrine. People in the classical Protestant tradition tend to regard more the role of the will, stressing a key moment of voluntary decision for Jesus, with an off-loading of guilt and the experience of personal salvation.

So, in general terms, Catholics are said to have a propositional faith while that of the classical Protestant is more experiential. Obviously these are very broad generalisations but they do indicate important differences of emphasis. Catholics tend to be uncomfortable if asked, 'Have you met the Lord Jesus ... are you saved? Have you been born again?' Whereas many Protestants are uncomfortable with authoritative definitions of dogmas of faith.

The balance of intellect and will should be sought. It is sad to meet a rigid, authoritarian orthodoxy which is immediately suspicious of religious experiences or emotional expressions. Some Catholics, on coming into contact with the Charismatic Renewal, spoke of the eighteen inch drop, meaning that their experience of God dropped from the brain into the heart. It is worth noting that the Latin term for believing, *credere,* literally means to give one's heart, *cor-dare.*

Yet the intellectual content of faith is absolutely vital. Lack of definition leads to all manner of confusion and compounds the scandal of Christian disunity. As Belloc observed, when the one pope is disregarded everyone tends to be their own pope. Because of the lack of recognised authority and clarity of definition, the sad fact is that the number of Christian sects is beyond counting. Some would estimate around thirty thousand and say that sects multiply at the rate of five per week.

If Jesus said that there would be only one flock ... if he prayed for unity among his disciples ... if he appointed Peter as the rock of the Church and the shepherd of the flock ... then surely there must be one orthodox teaching and one authoritative voice to declare that teaching.

According to the bible itself, it is the Church of God which is the pillar and the ground of truth (1 Tim 3:15).

The true believer comes into the light of Christ in saying *yes* to all the teaching of Jesus, by voluntarily entrusting one's life to the mercy and protection of God and by manifesting the fruits of

JOHN 3:1-21: ENCOUNTER WITH NICODEMUS

faith in a life of good works. This is the life of one born from above into supernatural life by the grace of God, voluntarily accepted.

Praying

Jesus, you came down from above to lift us up in divine adoption. No longer is it birth into a particular nation that matters for the call to the life of baptism is open to all nations. In the waters of baptism you breathe the Spirit of divine life into the soul.

After coming down, when your life on earth was complete you were lifted up: lifted up on the cross to show how much you loved us by taking on the wounds of sin due to us; and then, lifted up in your resurrection, you returned to the Father's glory.

May our lives be a constant *yes* to you, Jesus, Lord and Saviour.

ACCEPTING GOD'S LOVE

John 3:16-21.
> [16]Yes, God so loved the world that he gave his only Son that whoever believes in him may not be lost, but may have eternal life. [17]God did not send the Son into the world to condemn the world; instead, through him the world is to be saved. [18]Whoever believes in him will not be condemned. He who does not believe is already condemned because he has not believed in the Name of the only Son of God. [19]This is how the Judgement is made: Light has come into the world and people loved darkness rather than light because their deeds were evil. [20]For whoever does wrong hates the light and doesn't come to the light for fear that his deeds will be shown as evil. [21]But whoever lives according to the truth comes into the light so that it can be clearly seen that his works have been done in God.'

As the evangelist reflects on the words of Jesus to Nicodemus he expands further on two of his favourite themes:
  the love of God in sending down His Son;
  the part we play in accepting or rejecting what Jesus offers.

'Yes, God so loved the world that he gave his only Son that whoever believes in him may not be lost, but may have eternal life. God did not send the Son into the world to condemn the world; instead, through him the world is to be saved' (3:16-17). The term *world* is sometimes used in scripture as a name for unbelievers. But in this instance John is referring to the whole of God's creation. God loves his world. The world and its marvels did not come into being by chance or accident: it is the creation of God's wisdom and love.

Christians have not always been imbued with God's love for all created things. Sometimes an unbalanced asceticism associates enjoyment with guilt and puts a sad face on religion. John reminds us that the beginning and end of everything in life is God's love.

The love of God was shown above all when he sent his beloved Son to our world. His mission was not to condemn but to save; to be the way, the truth and the life; to be the true shepherd and the bread of life. Fullness of life was what he offered. Eternal life is our full potential as creatures made in the image and likeness of God. Why settle for anything less?

Sadly, sin gets a grip on people and, if allowed to poison the mind and heart, it leads away from the light of Christ. In allowing this drift from God to develop, people effectively are their own judges.

'This is how the Judgement is made: Light has come into the world and people loved darkness rather than light because their deeds were evil. But whoever lives according to the truth comes into the light so that it can be clearly seen that his works have been done in God' (Jn 3:19-21).

Many people ask how could a merciful God condemn anybody to hell. This text suggests that people will be their own judges. Whenever people reject the way of Jesus they are opting for the way of darkness. Once the sinner turns back to God in repentance, the God of love and mercy will take the sinner back. But if the sinner remains unrepentant, then the light of God will be something that the sinner will want to avoid.

The reason why people rejected Jesus and crucified him was their hatred for his light. Our eyes are made for light but if an eye is sore then the light will hurt it. Similarly, our stomachs are made for food, but if the tummy is sick, then even the mention of food will make it worse. In the same way, our souls are made for God, but if the soul is sick, then anything to do with God will be hated by that sick soul. The crucifixion of Jesus had its own sick logic.

The undisguised hatred of many of the critics of the church probably says more about the state of their own souls than about the church.

Praying

O God, the world is yours, created in your love and further sanctified in the incarnation. Your beloved Son took on earthly flesh and blood in a body nourished by the fruits of the earth. Fill us with a holy reverence for all that you have made. And may we never be so shortsighted as to see the works while forgetting the Maker.

Above all may we appreciate the love you showed in sending your Son to light our way to you. Bless us with a powerful faith which influences our hearts and enlightens our minds.

May we always look up to you and be lifted up to your bright glory. And by constant deeds of goodness may we manifest your love to the world.

John 3:22-36.
> ²²After this, Jesus went into the territory of Judea with his disciples. He stayed there with them and baptised. ²³John was also baptising in Aenon near Salim where water was plentiful; people came to him and were baptised. ²⁴(This happened before John was put in prison.) ²⁵Now John's disciples had been questioned by a Jew about spiritual cleansing, ²⁶so they came to him and said, 'Rabbi, the one who was with you across the Jordan, and about whom you spoke favourably, is now baptising and all are going to him.'
> ²⁷John answered, 'No one can take on anything if it has not been given him from heaven. ²⁸You yourselves are my witnesses that I said: "I am not the Christ but I have been sent before him."²⁹Only the bridegroom has the bride; but the friend of the bridegroom stands by and listens, and rejoices to hear the bridegroom's voice. My joy is now full. ³⁰It is necessary that he increase but that I decrease.

³¹He who comes from above is above all; he who comes from the earth belongs to the earth and his words, too, are earthly. The One who comes from heaven ³²speaks of the things he has seen and heard; he bears witness to this but no one accepts his testimony. ³³Yet whoever receives his testimony, acknowledges the truthfulness of God; ³⁴for God sent him and he speaks God's words and God gives him the Spirit without measure.
³⁵The Father loves the Son and has entrusted everything into his hands.
³⁶Whoever believes in the Son lives with eternal life, but he who will not believe in the Son will never know life and always faces the justice of God.'

For our reflection on John the Baptist, we refer the reader back to page 15.

John 4:1-42: The Samaritan Woman

After his encounters with the Jewish temple and then with Jewish teachers in the person of Nicodemus, now Jesus meets the Samaritans, a breakaway sect of Israel. The encounter with the Samaritan woman can be looked at on two levels: as an outreach of reconciliation with the Samaritans; and as an enthralling story of personal conversion.

> [1]The Pharisees heard that Jesus was attracting and baptizing more disciples than John, [2]although Jesus himself did not baptize but only his disciples. [3]When Jesus became aware of what was being said, he left Judea and returned to Galilee. [4]He had to cross Samaria. [5]He came to a Samaritan town called Sychar, near the land that Jacob had given to his son Joseph. [6]Jacob's well is there. Tired from his journey, Jesus sat down by the well; it was about noon. [7]Now a Samaritan woman came to draw water and Jesus said to her, 'Give me a drink.' [8]His disciples had just gone into town to buy some food.
> [9]The Samaritan woman said to him, 'How is it that you, a Jew, ask me, a Samaritan and a woman, for a drink?' (For Jews, in fact, have no dealings with Samaritans.) [10]Jesus replied, 'If you knew who it is that asks you for a drink, you yourself would have asked me and I would have given you living water.'
> [11]The woman answered, 'Sir, you have no bucket and this well is deep; where is your living water? [12]Are you greater than our ancestor Jacob, who gave us this well after he drank from it himself, together with his sons and his cattle?'
> [13]Jesus said to her, 'Whoever drinks of this water will be thirsty again; [14]but whoever drinks of the water that I shall give will never be thirsty; for the water that I shall give will become in him a spring of water welling up to eternal life.'
> [15]The woman said to him, 'Give me this water, that I may never be

thirsty and never have to come here to draw water.' ¹⁶Jesus said, 'Go, call your husband and come back here.' ¹⁷The woman answered, 'I have no husband.' And Jesus replied, 'You are right to say: 'I have no husband'; ¹⁸for you have had five husbands and the one you have now is not your husband. What you said is true.'

¹⁹The woman then said to him, 'I see you are a prophet; tell me this: ²⁰Our fathers used to come to this mountain to worship God; but you Jews, do you not claim that Jerusalem is the only place to worship God?'

²¹Jesus said to her, 'Believe me, woman, the hour is coming when you shall worship the Father, but that will not be on this mountain or in Jerusalem. ²²You Samaritans worship without knowledge, while we Jews worship with knowledge, for salvation comes from the Jews. ²³But the hour is coming and is even now here, when the true worshippers will worship the Father in spirit and truth; for that is the kind of worship the Father wants. ²⁴God is spirit and those who worship God must worship in spirit and truth.'

²⁵The woman said to him, 'I know that the Messiah, that is the Christ, is coming; when he comes, he will tell us everything.' ²⁶And Jesus said, 'I who am talking to you, I am he.'

²⁷At this point the disciples returned and were surprised that Jesus was speaking with a woman; however, no one said, 'What do you want?' or: 'Why are you talking with her?' ²⁸So the woman left her water jar and ran to the town. There she said to the people, ²⁹'Come and see a man who told me everything I did! Could he not be the Christ?' ³⁰So they left the town and went to meet him.

³¹In the meantime the disciples urged Jesus, 'Master, eat.' ³²But he said to them, 'I have food to eat that you don't know about.' ³³And the disciples wondered, 'Has anyone brought him food?' ³⁴Jesus said to them, 'My food is to do the will of the One who sent me and to carry out his work.

³⁵You say that in four more months it will be the harvest; now, I say to you, raise your eyes and see the fields white and ready for harvesting. ³⁶People who reap the harvest are paid for their work, and the fruit is gathered for eternal life, so that sower and reaper may rejoice together.

³⁷See the saying holds true: 'One sows and another reaps.' ³⁸I sent you to reap where you didn't work or suffer; others have worked and you are now sharing in their labours.'

³⁹In that town many Samaritans believed in him when they heard the woman who declared, 'He told me everything I did.' ⁴⁰So, when they came to him, they asked him to stay with them and Jesus

stayed there two days. [41]After that many more believed because of his words [42]and they said to the woman, 'We no longer believe because of what you told us; for we have heard for ourselves and we know that this is the Saviour of the world.'

The Samaritan Story

John frequently takes one person to represent many others. Just as Nicodemus represented the teachers of Israel, now the woman at the well represents the Samaritans who, in the eyes of the Jews, were schismatics or a breakaway splinter group.

Samaritans were the survivors of the ten Northern tribes who broke with the Southern tribes of Juda (Jews) and Benjamin in 931BC because of the excessive taxes levied for the building of the temple in Jerusalem. Two hundred years later, their kingdom was conquered by the Assyrians who planted the land with five pagan tribes, each with their own deity and religion. The worship of Yahweh was mixed up with five pagan religions (2 Kgs 17:24f.). The Samaritan woman represented her race in her five marriages and her present relationship did not merit the name of marriage, just as the pick-and-mix practices of her race did not deserve the name of worship.

The five husbands may also be a reference to the five books of the Law, the Pentateuch, the only part of the bible accepted by the Samaritans. They did not accept the Prophets or Wisdom literature which were written after their break-away. Indeed, the early prophets loudly condemned the pagan practices of the Northern Kingdom. Without the books of the Prophets, they awaited the coming of the great Prophet promised by Moses in Deuteronomy 18:18. We can see now how loaded with meaning is the woman's recognition of Jesus as a prophet.

Places of worship were an unending bone of contention. The original split occurred over taxation for the Jerusalem temple. When the Jews returned from Babylon and started to rebuild the temple, the Samaritans offered help. But no way would the Jews accept the help of contaminated hands (Ezra 4). Later the Samaritans set up a rival shrine on Mount Gerizim but this was destroyed by the Maccabees. The woman reminded Jesus of the ancient Jewish hostility towards Samaritan worship. But Jesus had come to transcend the divisions and prejudices of history.

On this level, the story is another instance of how Jesus replaced the legacy of the Jewish past. His encounter with the woman and then with the people of the town marked the dissolution of ancient divisions and acrimony.

Story of the Woman
On the level of personal conversion it is a marvellous story of God's outreach. We can recognise the personal barriers that the woman had to break through.

The portrait of Jesus here is most appealing. At the start of the story he is tired and thirsty, glad to have a place to sit down. Who could be afraid of a God like that?

If we were asked what is God like in this episode, we might answer: God breaks down prejudices ... God is forgiving ... knows our past yet accepts us ... understands everything ... searches for the lonely and the lost ... leads to worship.

Rising Titles
It is worth noticing the different titles by which the woman addresses Jesus. John's stories rise up like the song of the skylark.

Initially we hear her almost spit out the hated name Jew. But later, once Jesus has shown her the courtesy of speaking kindly with her, she calls him Sir. As the story develops, she couples him in the same breath as our father, Jacob, the first Israelite and father of Jews and Samaritans alike. Samaritans did not accept the books of the prophets but awaited the prophet promised at the time of Moses, so when she recognises Jesus as prophet, it is a very high title indeed. Eventually she wonders if he might be the Messiah. By the end of the story, Jesus is recognised as the saviour of the world.

Waters of Life
Keeping pace with the rising recognition of Jesus is the interior conversion of the woman. Since it begins as a story about water and thirst, it invites us to trace the different levels of thirst in her life.

Her first thirst is for personal acceptance, the foundation of human dignity. It is significant that she came to the well alone and at the sixth hour, midday. Coming to the well was the one chance the women had of getting out of the house and having a chat together. But they normally avoided the warmest time of day. It seems that this woman was unpopular in town, quite understandable given her marital history.

She had been betrayed in religion because in her experience it set people at enmity with one another. Nor had she fared any better in her love-life. Bearing the legacy of five broken relationships, she could no longer trust anybody or believe in fidelity.

Socially outcast, betrayed and bruised, now she met Jesus at the well. She knew that a Jew should not speak to a Samaritan and that a Rabbi should never speak to a woman alone. But everything changed once he spoke to her and asked her for a drink. Obviously Jesus was different. This bruised woman before him was more important than the bitter fruits of history. She felt accepted. It was balm to her wounded memory.

Her second thirst was for forgiveness. Jesus led her on to recognise the deeper, inner thirsts of life: those nagging areas of dissatisfaction and discontentment. He said that he would give the gift of an inner spring of water to satisfy these deeper thirsts. Later in the story, when she called out the townspeople to meet Jesus, she said of him that he told her everything about herself. Everything? Well, not in minute detail, but in a way that she had felt totally understood and accepted.

'I wonder if he is the Christ,' she said.

To understand all is to forgive. Only God has the total understanding of every detail of our lives. Only God has the creating and re-creating love to offer total forgiveness. She felt the weight of the past and all its diminishment being lifted from her.

Having encountered God, her third thirst was for a way of worship. Worship belongs to the soul's thirst for transcendence, for something that goes beyond the grave and is greater than life as we know it.

C.S. Lewis wrote about the God-shaped emptiness in the human heart: a jigsaw that is not complete without God. Saint Augustine, after many years of searching, concluded that the soul is made for God and will know no rest until it rests in God. But for this woman the minefield of historical contention had to be negotiated.

Jesus went beyond the shrines and mountains of history to the idea of true worship, worship of the Father, in spirit and in truth. Christian readers will here see a reference to the Blessed Trinity, for the spirit is the Holy Spirit and the truth resides in Jesus, the Word of the Father. True worship is a participation in the inner life of the Triune God, a return of glory to the Father, through the Son, in the power of the Holy Spirit. The most perfect form of worship here on earth is to participate in the Eucharistic Prayer. 'Through Jesus, with him and in him, in the unity of the Holy Spirit, all glory and honour is yours, almighty Father, for ever and ever.'

Connecting

The Catechism of the Catholic Church takes up this picture of the woman at the well to illustrate a very important truth about prayer. Prayer begins, not so much in our giving time to God, but in God's thirst for us.

'"If you knew the gift of God!" The wonder of prayer is revealed beside the well where we come seeking water: there, Christ comes to meet every human being. It is he who first seeks us and asks us for a drink. Jesus thirsts; his asking arises from the depths of God's thirst for us. Whether we realise it or not, prayer is the encounter of God's thirst with ours. God thirsts that we may thirst for him' (CCC 2560).

We are inclined to think of prayer as the time that we make available to God. Basically, we regard it as something we do, when we decide. We must grow in the realisation that God is reaching out to us twenty-four hours of the day, not just when we set a little time aside.

God is waiting at the well for us, thirsting for our presence. All he asks of us is the empty bucket of our lives. It is God who can supply the living water.

In the wonder of the incarnation, God loved us and came among us, to sit beside us in our emptiness and loneliness, our disappointments and sorrows, our fears and anxieties, our hopes and aspirations, our joys and celebrations.

Jesus will lead us to the truth because he is the true prophet.

The Holy Spirit is waiting to fill our hearts with a huge experience of divine love. In the power of the Spirit we enter into the liturgy of divine life, rendering glory and honour to the Father, through and in Jesus Christ, his Son.

Praying

O Lord Jesus, you sit down beside us as we come to the well to slake our thirst. And in your presence everything is changed. You pay attention to us, you accept us, you restore our dignity as God's children.

You read us like an open book. At first it is embarrassing, but then it brings great relief, for your love transcends our sinfulness. We no longer have to hide, for you know us totally and yet you love us all the more.

How amazing, that you, the maker of all things should ask us for the use of our empty bucket! That you, the provider of eternal fountains, should need a drink!

What you really thirst for is an empty, humble heart into which you can pour the living waters of the Holy Spirit.

You lead us beyond our guilt and unworthiness to the mountain heights of divine worship.

O Jesus, through you, with you and in you, in the unity of the Holy Spirit, all glory and honour to the Father.

John 4:43-54: The Second Sign

[43]When the two days were over Jesus left for Galilee. [44]Jesus himself said that no prophet is recognized in his own country. [45]Yet the Galileans welcomed him when he arrived, because of all the things he had done in Jerusalem during the Festival and which they had seen. For they, too, had gone to the feast.
[46]Jesus went back to Cana of Galilee where he had changed the water into wine. At Capernaum there was an official whose son was ill [47]and when he heard that Jesus had come from Judea to Galilee, he went and asked for him to come and heal his son, for he was at the point of death.
[48]Jesus said, 'Unless you see signs and wonders, you will not believe!' [49]The official said, 'Sir, come down before my child dies.' [50]And Jesus replied, 'Go, your son is living.'
The man had faith in the word that Jesus spoke to him and went his way.
[51]He was already going down the hilly road when his servants met him with this news, 'Your son has recovered!' [52]So he asked them at what hour the child had begun to recover and they said to him, 'The fever left him yesterday in the afternoon about one o'clock.' [53]And the father realized that it was the time when Jesus told him, 'Your son is living.' And he became a believer, he and all his family.
[54]Jesus performed this second miraculous sign when he returned from Judea to Galilee.

The court official from Capernaum is not named. From the parallel story in Luke 7 we know that he was a Gentile. This one, unnamed Gentile, represents all those from pagan backgrounds who had professed faith in Jesus by the time John was writing.

Having heard about Jesus, this court official went to him in desperate plea for his sick son. The reply of Jesus comes as a jolt. 'So you will not believe unless you see signs and wonders!'

JOHN 4:43-54: THE SECOND SIGN

These words are hardly a criticism of the official who had come in faith but more a comment on the superficial level of faith among the people. Jesus wanted to shock them into a deeper level of thinking.

The official humbly repeated his urgent request. The reply of Jesus carried the weight of divine authority. 'Go home, your son will live.'

The official believed the word of Jesus and set out on his journey home. This journey, which was inspired by the word of Jesus, represents the pilgrimage of faith. Through the darkness of night he travelled towards home, not knowing until the following day that God had already blessed him with the answer to his prayer.

It was at the seventh hour that he had received the word of Jesus, one hour later than the encounter of the Samaritan woman. The time factor represents an advance in faith. So, we are told that he and all his household became believers.

This was the second sign given by Jesus. Like the first sign, it was given at Cana. John intends the reader to treat the section between the two signs as a unit. The first sign, the changing of water into wine, symbolised the complete renewal of the old religion. This was followed by the replacement of the Jerusalem temple. Jesus then proceeded to reach out to orthodox Jews in the person of the teacher, Nicodemus; next to the schismatic Samaritans; and thirdly to the pagan nations as represented in the court official. The reaction is very positive for he and all his household believed.

Connecting

This is a story about journeys and about faith. Jesus travelled from the place where there was no respect for a prophet and no faith, to the place where he was well received.

The journey of the court official was from Cana to Capernaum, about thirty miles, a fair journey in those times. He set out at the seventh hour, one in the afternoon, to travel through the night on strength of the word of Jesus. He reminds one of

Abraham, the model of believers, who set out from his father's house on a life's journey into the unknown, on strength of a promise from God. His journey brought him through ten testings and seven promises of blessing. The court official travelled through the night before he received confirmation of his blessing on the morrow.

In the words of Pope John Paul II, 'to believe is to abandon oneself to the truth of the word of the living God, knowing and humbly recognising how unsearchable are his judgements and how inscrutable his ways.'

Legend has it that in the Exodus the Red Sea did not part until the people obeyed Moses and stepped into the water. The authenticity of one's faith is not known until one has to step into the darkness.

We connect with the story in the way that it jolts us into thinking about the depth of our faith. This story shows that faith must have a deeper foundation than fascination with miracles. It demands a process of growth from merely using God to taking God on his terms.

On a superficial level, one may believe in God because of the many consolations it brings – forgiveness, peace, access to miracles and heaven at the end. It is the greatest form of insurance policy. This faith, if it goes no deeper, will not survive unless it is constantly receiving assurance by stories of signs and wonders. People with this sort of faith are attracted to groups where witnessing to the favours of God dominates all else.

A superficial faith is like the seed that grows on shallow soil. It survives as long as it gets regular watering. But a dry spell will test whether the roots are deep enough. Dryness in prayer will be a severe testing of shallow faith. A great mystical writer, Meister Eckhart, warned that to use God is to kill him. If I use God simply to serve my own needs, then I have to admit that the god I worship is myself. Then my prayer is not 'Thy will be done' but 'My will be done'. If we believe in the Jesus of glory on the mountain, we must also believe in him while in agony in Gethsemane.

Regularly we say prayers which express our trust in God. But from what level of conviction are these words coming? Events or happenings may jolt us and test whether there is a lasting depth in our trust. If we survive the testing, our faith will have been purified. In daylight we can see all the objects nearby. But it is only in the dark of night that we can see the distant stars. When God asks us to travel into the night on strength of his promise, it is to deepen our faith by purifying it of self-gratification.

Praying

We believe, Lord, help our unbelief.

O God, may we hear your word with the same confidence that the court official showed.

When you call us to step into the darkness, may your promise be sufficient support to keep us going.

We pray for all who are going through a time of dryness and darkness. May it be for them a journey away from selfish preoccupation to a more pure faith. May their eyes be drawn to the distant stars.

Your word, O Lord, is light for our journey and the source of our hope.

John 5:1-47: Healing on the Sabbath

The Paralysed Man

[1]After this there was a feast of the Jews and Jesus went up to Jerusalem. [2]Now, by the Sheep Gate in Jerusalem, there is a pool (called Bethzatha in Hebrew) surrounded by five galleries. [3]In these galleries lay a multitude of sick people – blind, lame and paralyzed – [4]waiting for the water to move. For at times an angel of the Lord would have a swim into the pool and stir up the water; and the first person to enter after this movement of the water would be healed of whatever disease he had.
[5]There was a man who had been sick for thirty-eight years. [6]Jesus saw him and since he knew how long this man had been lying there, he said to him, 'Do you want to be healed?' [7]And the sick man answered, 'Sir, I have no one to put me into the pool when the water is disturbed; so while I am still on the way, another steps down before me.'
[8]Jesus then said to him, 'Rise, take up your mat and walk.' [9]And at once the man was healed, and he took up his mat and walked.

Now that day happened to be the sabbath. [10]So the Jews said to the man who had just been healed, 'It is the sabbath and the Law doesn't allow you to carry your mat.' [11]He answered them, 'The one who healed me said to me: Take up your mat and walk.' [12]They asked him, 'Who is the one who said to you: Take up you mat and walk?' [13]But the sick man had no idea who it was who had cured him, for Jesus had slipped away among the crowd that filled the place.

[14]Afterwards Jesus found him in the Temple court and told him, 'Now you are well; don't sin again lest something worse happen to you.' [15]And the man went back and told the Jews that it was Jesus who had healed him.

This is a story about illness and healing. The man at the pool suffered from some crippling ailment. But it is also an event to be seen on the larger canvas of the whole Jewish story.

Just as the woman at the well who represented the Samaritans was not named, neither is this crippled representative of the Jews named. She, with her five marriages, represented the pagan alliances of the Samaritans. This crippled Jew beside the water in Jerusalem represents something of Jewish history. The number once again provides the link. For thirty-eight years he lay beside the waters of healing, unable to enter. This was exactly the duration of the exodus of their forebears before they entered the waters of the Jordan to cross over into the promised land.

'We walked for thirty-eight years from Kadesh-Barnea until we crossed the brook, until the entire generation of men old enough to fight had perished just as Yahweh said' (Deut 2:14). These fighting men were excluded from entering the land because they had lost faith in God being at their side, thinking that their own fighting prowess was all that they could rely on (cf. Deut 1:35). The wandering people were doomed to remain in the wilderness until all who had doubted God had died.

Representing the unbelieving Jews of his time, this crippled man lay for thirty-eight years, unable to enter the waters of healing to cross into his land of health and happiness.

As John wrote up the story he probably intended its application to the Jews of his own time of writing who did not believe in Jesus. He lamented that they had not entered into the waters of baptism to pass over into the fullness of life that Jesus brings. They were still wandering in the wilderness of unbelief.

Connecting

As in the story of the woman at the well, it was Jesus who took the initiative. It sounds like asking the obvious: 'Do you want to be healed?' Why on earth was he coming to this pool every day unless he hoped to be healed?

But Jesus knew what he was saying. It is significant that the crippled man did not give a direct answer. Notice that he started portioning blame. 'I have no one to put me in ... others get in before me.' All negative thinking. Poor little old me! Call it PLOM for short. This man was suffering from a massive dose of PLOM.

As an antidote to this disease, Jesus prescribed a triple action. His voice is strong, his authority clear. 'Stand up, take up your mat and walk.' If this ailment came from negative thinking then the healing must come from a positive attitude. Later on, when Jesus met him in the Temple court, he warned him not to go back to his negative way or he would be worse off than before. A relapse is usually worse than the original condition. Just ask the alcoholic or the smoker.

The story challenges me to examine my own PLOM rating. To what extent do I hold on to negative memories, or engage in negative thinking? Is it my custom to put the blame on others ... they get in before me .. nobody helps me ... nobody understands me?

Psychologists recognise how much self-pity allows people to engage in compensatory behaviour. They refer to it as secondary gain. People will justify excessive eating or drinking or immoral behaviour on the grounds that they are entitled to take some bit of pleasure in a world where nobody understands.

Secondary gain offers an excuse for laziness, for lack of initiative, for not taking responsibility. The sleeping-mat is an image of self-pity. Watch how a tired child whose world gets very self-centred wants to clutch a comfy blanket or a cuddly toy.

The words of Jesus are strong: 'Stand up, take up your mat and walk.' They are at once a command and an encouragement.

Praying

O Jesus, you are the Beloved Son and equal of the Father. Yet you are ever at our side in our exodus-journey of life to the promised land.

There are times when we forget you and doubt your help, thinking that we have only our own powers to trust in. Then we are dragged down into negative thinking. We take out our own inner frustration in blaming others. Poor, little old me. Nobody understands, nobody puts me into the waters of life.

Lord, forgive our doubts.

May we draw strength from hearing your command to stand up, to let go of selfish comforts and to walk the journey of today.

The Sabbath Controversy

John 5:16-47.

¹⁶So the Jews persecuted Jesus because he performed healings like this on the sabbath.

¹⁷Jesus replied, 'My Father goes on working and so do I.' ¹⁸And the Jews wished all the harder to kill him, for Jesus not only broke the sabbath observance but also made himself equal with God, calling him his own Father.

¹⁹Jesus said to them, 'Truly, I assure you the Son cannot do anything by himself, but only what he sees the Father does. And whatever he does, the Son also does. ²⁰The Father loves the Son and shows him everything he does; and he will show him even greater things than these, so that you will be amazed.

²¹As the Father raises the dead and gives them life, so the Son gives life to whom he wills. ²²In the same way the Father judges no one, for he has entrusted to the Son all judgement, ²³and he wants all to honour the Son as they honour the Father. Whoever ignores the Son, ignores as well the Father who sent him.

²⁴Truly, I say to you, he who hears my word and believes him who sent me, has eternal life; and there is no judgement for him because he has passed from death to life.

²⁵Truly, the hour is coming and has indeed come, when the dead will hear the voice of the Son of God and, on hearing it, will live. ²⁶For the Father has life in himself and he has given to the Son also to have life in himself. ²⁷And he has empowered him as well to carry out Judgement, for he is a son of man.

²⁸Do not be surprised at this: the hour is coming when all those lying in tombs will hear my voice ²⁹and come out; those who have done good shall rise to live, and those who have done evil will rise to be condemned.

³⁰I can do nothing of myself, and I need to hear Another One to judge; and my own judgement is just, because I seek not my own will, but the will of him who sent me.

³¹If I bore witness to myself, my testimony would be worthless. ³²But Another One is bearing witness to me and I know that his testimony of me is true. ³³John also bore witness to the truth when you sent messengers to him, ³⁴but I do not seek such human testimony; I recall this for you, so that you may be saved.

[35]John was a burning and shining lamp and, for a while, you were willing to enjoy his light. [36]But I have greater evidence than that of John – the works which the Father entrusted to me to carry out. The very works I do prove that the Father has sent me. [37]Thus he who bears witness to me is the Father who sent me. You have never heard his voice and have never seen his likeness; [38]then, as long as you do not believe his messenger, his word is not in you.
[39]You search in the Scriptures and you think that in them you will find life; yet it is to me that Scripture refers. [40]But you refuse to come to me, that you may live. [41]I am not seeking the praise of men [42]but I have known that love of God is not within you. [43]Even though I have come in my Father's name, you do not accept me; but if another comes in his own name, you will accept him. [44]As long as you seek praise from one another instead of seeking the Glory coming from the only God, how can you believe?
[45]Do not think that I shall accuse you to the Father. Moses himself in whom you place your hope, accuses you. [46]If you believed Moses, you would believe me, for he wrote of me. [47]But if you do not believe what he wrote, how will you believe what I say?

Jesus came to change the waters of purification into wine to celebrate the wedding of heaven and earth. As a result of this linking of heaven and earth which he had promised to Nathanael, various Jewish institutions had to be replaced. The temple would be replaced by worship in the risen Lord. Birth into Jewish lineage would be replaced by the new life of faith. The ancient division with Samaritans would be transcended in the new worship in spirit and in truth. That is the story so far.

The focus shifts now to the great Jewish feasts. From Chapter 5 to Chapter 12 four feasts occur and in each case Jesus develops a new meaning to the celebration.

The first feast is the Sabbath. Because it was a Sabbath when Jesus healed the crippled man, controversy erupted. It was serious stuff. As the arguments developed, the Jews considered it a case for the death penalty because Jesus not only broke a Sabbath regulation but he spoke of God as his own Father, and so made himself God's equal.

The Sabbath was the oldest feast, going back to the account of the first week of creation. 'And God blessed the seventh day and

JOHN 5:1-47: HEALING ON THE SABBATH

made it holy, because on that day he rested from all the work he had done in his creation' (Gen 2:3).

God's rest did not mean that he closed shop every Saturday. Otherwise creation would cease to be sustained, planets would stop revolving, nothing would grow. Jewish Rabbis recognised three essential works of God which continued on the Sabbath – birth, judgement and resurrection.

Jesus picked up on this idea. 'My Father goes on working and so do I' (5:17). In the best Jewish tradition of a son learning his trade from his father, Jesus pointed out that the works he was performing were the same as what the Father did on the Sabbath.

Birth: he was bringing new life to the world.

Judgement: by their reaction to his words people were passing judgement on themselves.

Resurrection: he is the source of eternal life.

The controversy continues like a court case. From verses 31 to 47, Jesus calls up the witnesses on his behalf: John the Baptist, the witness of his works, the testimony of scripture and of Moses. Jesus has stated his case.

Connecting

Jesus had many clashes with the Pharisees over the spirit and meaning of the Sabbath. The heavy hand of legalism placed so much emphasis on the prohibitions that they lost sight of the celebration of family, community and God. The original Sabbath day of rest was a contemplative enjoyment of creation, time to savour and enjoy the produce of the week.

An outstanding Rabbi of today, Jonathan Sacks, has written meditatively about his experience of Sabbath. 'The Sabbath is our moment of eternity in the midst of time. Within the cycle of the week it creates a delicate rhythm of action and reflection, making and enjoying, running and standing still. Without that pause to experience family, community and God we risk making the journey while missing the view.' (Sacks, *Faith in the Future*, DLT, p. 137)

The early Christians soon distanced themselves from the pharisaic Sabbath. They changed the focus from Saturday to Sunday. Sunday was celebrated as the first day of creation, the day of resurrection and the day of Pentecost. They saw it as the day of the Father creating, the Son rising and the Holy Spirit descending. 'O day of life and light and grace, from earthly toil a dwelling place' (Breviary hymn).

But Sunday is also the seventh day, the time set apart after the work of the week. It is an anticipation of the eternal rest when this life's toil is completed. We must not lose sight of the contemplative aspect of the Lord's day. 'On Sundays and other holy days of obligation, the faithful are to refrain from engaging in work or activities that hinder the worship owed to God, the joy proper to the Lord's Day, the performance of works of mercy, and the appropriate relaxation of mind and body' (CCC 2185).

Sunday is a day to find more time to be in touch with the depths of our creation, to celebrate the Lord's resurrection and to be more attentive in spiritual activities to the breath of the Holy Spirit. When we are more in touch with the depths of God in our inner selves, then we will be more relaxed with family or community, and we will be more available to the corporal works of mercy like visiting the sick or lonely.

Saint Augustine gave beautiful expression to the holy restfulness of the Lord's Day.

We shall rest and we shall see.
We shall see and we shall love.
We shall love and we shall praise.

The Lord's Day invites us to soul-time, family-time and God-time. As Jesus emphasised, it is a day of celebrating his presence among us.

Praying

O God, we get so caught up in living that we forget you who are the source of life.

We thank you for Sabbath, a holy day of rest, a day to stand back and regain our perspective. We thank you for the Christian

JOHN 5:1-47: HEALING ON THE SABBATH

Sunday, a day to celebrate creation, resurrection and the outpouring of the Holy Spirit.

We humbly ask you to enrich our Sunday Sabbath. May it be for us a day of true worship: a day to know you in the scriptures; a day with time for one another in family and community; a day to remember the sick and lonely.

O God of the weekdays, may we celebrate you on Sunday. O God of our Sundays, strengthen us for the week ahead.

John 6:1-71: The Bread of Life

The New Passover
The sixth chapter is by far the longest in the gospel. After developing the meaning of the weekly feast of Sabbath in the last chapter, the focus shifts to the great annual feast of Passover. In the liturgical context of the Passover, Jesus identifies himself as the bread of life come down from heaven. It is a key chapter as reactions to the words of Jesus divide the people into unbelievers and believers. John develops the chapter in three sections:
Verses 1-21: The miraculous signs of Jesus.
Verses 22-58: The discourse arising from these signs.
Verses 59-71: The reactions of unbelief and belief.

1. The Miraculous Signs
[1]After this Jesus went to the other side of the Sea of Galilee, near Tiberias, [2]and large crowds followed him because of the miraculous signs they saw when he healed the sick. [3]So he went up into the hills and sat down there with his disciples. [4]Now the Passover, the feast of the Jews, was at hand.
[5]Then lifting up his eyes, Jesus saw the crowds that were coming to him and said to Philip, 'Where shall we buy bread so that these people may eat?' [6]He said this to test Philip, for he himself knew what he was to do. [7]Philip answered him, 'Two hundred silver coins would not buy enough bread for each of them to have a piece.'
[8]Then one of the disciples spoke to Jesus. Andrew, Simon Peter's brother, said, [9]'There is a boy here who has five barley loaves and two fish; but what good are these for so many?'
[10]Jesus said, 'Make the people sit down.' There was plenty of grass there so the people, about five thousand men, sat down to rest. [11]Jesus then took the loaves, gave thanks and distributed them to those who were seated. He did the same with the fish and gave

them as much as they wanted. ¹²And when they had eaten enough, he told his disciples, 'Gather up the pieces left over, that nothing may be lost.'
¹³So they gathered them up and filled twelve baskets with bread, that is with pieces of the five barley loaves left by those who had eaten.
¹⁴When the people saw this sign that Jesus had just given, they said, 'This is really the Prophet, he who is come into the world.' ¹⁵Jesus realized that they would come and take him by force to make him king; so he fled to the hills by himself.
¹⁶When evening came, the disciples went down to the shore. ¹⁷After a while they got into a boat to make for Capernaum on the other side of the sea for it was now dark and Jesus had not yet come to them. ¹⁸But the sea was getting rough because a strong wind was blowing.
¹⁹They had rowed about three or four miles, when they saw Jesus walking on the sea, and he was drawing near to the boat. They were frightened, ²⁰but he said to them, 'It is I; do not be afraid.'
²¹They wanted to take him into the boat, but immediately the boat was at the shore to which they were going.

'The Passover, the feast of the Jews, was at hand.' This liturgical setting is very important in understanding the deep meaning of the chapter. Later in the gospel John will make it very clear that the death of Jesus took place at the same time-setting, just before the Passover of the Jews. What Jesus says in this chapter about the Bread of Life cannot be fully understood without connecting it with the final Passover when he passed from this world to the Father.

The Passover commemorated the journey from slavery to freedom under the leadership of Moses. It was the event which moulded the Israelite people into a nation with an identity and a land of their own.

The annual Passover memorial celebrated two great deeds of God – the miraculous crossing of the Red Sea and the supply of manna to feed the people. In a double Passover sign Jesus fed the people and, having miraculously walked across the stormy sea, he brought the boats of the disciples safely to land in no time.

There are several strands of connection with Moses. The mention of Jesus climbing the hill is a reminder of Moses going up Mount Sinai. After the people had been fed by Jesus they called him the Prophet, referring to the one who had been promised by God through the mouth of Moses. When Jesus spoke there were loud murmurs of disbelief, recalling the grumbling and murmurs of many during the Exodus.

By making such obvious connections with the Exodus and its annual celebration at Passover, John is clearly setting the context for a development of the new meaning to be assigned to the Passover. But it will not be fully understood until the final Passover.

Certain words and phrases used here have eucharistic connotations. The actions at Eucharist are echoed as Jesus took the loaves, gave thanks and distributed them. The Greek word used here for giving thanks is *eucharistesas*. The words for gathering and fragments were used with eucharistic associations in the *Didache*, a teaching document which predates John's gospel.

2. The Discourse

22Next day the people who had stayed on the other side realised that only one boat had been there and that Jesus had not entered it with his disciples; rather, the disciples had gone away alone. 23Bigger boats from Tiberius came near the place where all these people had eaten the bread. 24So, when they saw that neither Jesus nor his disciples were there, they got into the boats and went to Capernaum looking for Jesus.
25When they found him on the other side of the lake, they asked him, 'Master, when did you come here?'
26Jesus answered, 'Truly, I say to you, you look for me, not because of the signs you have seen, but because you ate bread and were satisfied. 27Work then, not for perishable food, but for the lasting food which gives eternal life. This is the food that the Son of Man gives to you, for the Father's seal has been put on him.'
28Then the Jews asked him, 'What shall we do? What are the works that God wants us to do?' 29And Jesus answered them, 'The work God wants is this: that you believe in the One whom God has sent.'
30They then said, 'Show us miraculous signs, that we may see and believe you. What sign do you perform?' 31Our fathers are manna in

JOHN 6:1-71: THE BREAD OF LIFE

the desert; as Scripture says: They were given bread from heaven to eat.'

32Jesus then said to them, 'Truly, I say to you, it was not Moses who gave you the bread from heaven. My Father gives you the true bread from heaven. 33The bread God gives is the One who comes from heaven and gives life to the world.' 34And they said to him, 'Give us this bread always.'

35Jesus said to them, 'I am the bread of life; he who comes to me shall never be hungry, and he who believes in me shall never be thirsty. 36Nevertheless, as I said, you refuse to believe, even when you have seen. 37Yet, all that the Father gives me will come to me, and whoever comes to me, I shall not turn away. 38For I have come from heaven, not to do my own will, but the will of the One who sent me.

39And the will of him who sent me is that I lose nothing of what he has given me, but instead that I raise it up on the last day. 40This is the will of the Father, that whoever sees the Son and believes in him shall live with eternal life; and I will raise him up on the last day.'

41The Jews murmured because Jesus has said, 'I am the bread which comes from heaven.' 42And they said, 'This man is the son of Joseph, isn't he? We know his father and mother. How can he say that he has come from heaven?'

43Jesus answered them, 'Do not murmur among yourselves. 44No one can come to me unless he is drawn by the Father who sent me; and I will raise him up on the last day. 45It has been written in the Prophets: They shall all be taught by God. So whoever listens and learns from the Father comes to me.

46For no one has seen the Father except the One who comes from God; he has seen the Father. 47Truly, I say to you, he who believes has eternal life.

48I am the bread of life. 49Though your ancestors ate the manna in the desert, they died. 50But here you have the bread which comes from heaven so that you may eat of it and not die.

51I am the living bread which has come from heaven; whoever eats of this bread will live forever. The bread I shall give is my flesh and I will give it for the life of the world.'

52The Jews were arguing among themselves, 'How can this man give us flesh to eat?' 53So Jesus replied, 'Truly, I say to you, if you do not eat the flesh of the Son of Man and drink his blood, you have no life in you. 54He who eats my flesh and drinks my blood lives with eternal life and I will raise him up on the last day.

55My flesh is really food and my blood is drink. 56He who eats my flesh and drinks my blood, lives in me and I in him. ⁵⁷Just as the Father, who is life, sent me and I have life from the Father, so he who eats me will have life from me. ⁵⁸This is the bread which came from Heaven; unlike that of your ancestors, who ate and later died. He who eats this bread will live forever.'

The multiplication of the loaves and fishes is recognised by the people as a sign given by Jesus (6:14). When we reach a road sign we do not stay there but we take direction and move on. The miraculous deeds of Jesus in this gospel are signs which invite people to move on to a deeper meaning. Feeding the bodily hunger of the people pointed to the desire of Jesus to feed also their spiritual hungers. 'Truly, I say to you, you look for me, not because of the signs you have seen, but because you ate bread and were satisfied. Work then, not for perishable food, but for the lasting food which gives eternal life. This is the food that the Son of Man gives to you, for the Father's seal has been put on him' (6:26-27). The seal is like the baker's name or trademark which we used to see on loaves of bread in the days before sliced pans.

'What are the works that God wants of us?,' they ask.

'The work God wants is this: that you believe in the One whom God has sent.' They catch the implications of this: that Jesus is claiming to be the One sent by God. They want to see a sign as proof of his claim, recalling the sign of the manna at the time of Moses.

Jesus takes up the wonder of the manna. One feature of that food was that it lasted no more than a day. The sort of food that Jesus offers in not only for today's needs but for the needs of every day and for all time. And he *is* that bread. 'I am the bread of life; he who comes to me shall never be hungry, and he who believes in me shall never be thirsty' (6:35). He is speaking of the hungers of mind and heart. The mind is made to pursue truth and the heart hungers for a love that is faithful and true. In the wisdom of his word, Jesus is the bread to satisfy this hunger of the heart and thirst of the mind.

JOHN 6:1-71: THE BREAD OF LIFE

The bread of his word

The Old Testament had used the imagery of hunger and thirst with reference to the gift of wisdom. 'Those who eat me will hunger still, those who drink me will thirst for more' (Sir 24:21). The water from the well in Samaria did not give eternal satisfaction whereas the water that Jesus promised would be an undying satisfaction. Similarly, the wisdom of the Old Testament writer did not promise eternal food and drink but the teaching word of Jesus did promise eternal satisfaction.

Roman emperors sought to distract the minds of people from their social injustices by placating them with bread and circus. Nowadays consumerism and changing fashions create hollow needs which obscure the serious searchings of life. Entertainment has become the highest paid profession in an effort to distract the restless mind. The deception inherent in today's shallow living has borne poisoned fruit in restlessness, loneliness, impermanent relationships, dependence on chemical support, suicides, and a wide menu of outlandish beliefs in such substitutes as astral powers, the spirit of trees or the power of stones.

Belief in Jesus is the way to eternal life, to a life which transcends death, to values that are permanent, to a meaning which holds all the parts of life in unity. The centre holds fast, the foundation is firm and that house is not swept away.

Belief is firstly a grace from the Father. 'No one can come to me unless drawn by the Father who sent me' (6:44).

Secondly, this grace comes through the teaching of Jesus.

Then, thirdly, it must be accepted in personal faith.

'Whoever listens and learns from the Father comes to me. For no one has seen the Father. The One who comes from God has seen the Father. Truly, I say to you, he who believes has eternal life' (6:45-47). The words of Jesus express the eternal wisdom of God, food of eternal satisfaction.

The bread of his flesh

The words of Jesus change direction in 6:51. Up to this he has been speaking of the bread he has given, namely his teaching word. But now he changes to the future tense and speaks of 'the bread that I shall give.' What is this future bread? It is 'my flesh and I will give it for the life of the world.' As we have noted above, the gift of wisdom was spoken of in the Old Testament under the imagery of eating and drinking but never under the images of flesh and blood. At this point Jesus is moving on the discourse to something beyond the wisdom of his word. He is taking the story up to a higher level of belief. This, of course, is but another instance of how John develops ideas by rising to higher planes of thought.

The Greek word for eating recorded by John is one that expressed audible munching. It was a shocking, revolting expression to a people who had such strict laws about drawing off all blood from meat. The language of Jesus was intended to shock because it anticipates his sacrificial death and the blood he was to shed as the sealing of the new covenant. The liturgical context of the Passover enables the reader to connect these words with the death of Jesus which took place, according to John, as the Passover lambs were being sacrificed.

The Jews began to argue about giving his flesh to eat. Rather than withdraw his statement, Jesus reaffirmed it five times with slight variations. 'My flesh is really food and my blood is drink. He who eats my flesh and drinks my blood, lives in me and I in him' (6:55-56).

Connecting

From the earliest times, Christians have connected these words with the accounts of the institution of the Eucharist in the synoptic gospels and the First Letter of Paul to the Corinthians.

The celebration of the Eucharist is the meal of the new covenant, the fulfilment of the Passover, the celebration of Jesus returning to the Father. There are two tables in the celebration, the table of the word and the table of the bread and wine. These correspond to Jesus as the bread of life in his teaching (6:35-50) and in his flesh and blood given up for the life of the world (6:51-58).

JOHN 6:1-71: THE BREAD OF LIFE

3. Unbelief and Belief

⁵⁹Thus did Jesus speak in Capernaum when he taught them in the synagogue.

⁶⁰After hearing this, many of Jesus' followers said, 'This sort of teaching is very hard! Who can accept it?'

⁶¹Jesus was aware that his disciples were murmuring about this and so he said to them, 'Does this offend you? ⁶²Then, how will you react when you see the Son of Man ascending to where he was before? ⁶³It is the spirit that gives life; the flesh cannot help. The words that I have spoken to you are spirit and they are life. ⁶⁴Yet among you there are some who do not believe.'

From the beginning, Jesus knew who would betray him. ⁶⁵So he added, 'As I have told you, no one can come to me unless it is given to him by the Father.'

⁶⁶After this many disciples withdrew and no longer followed him. ⁶⁷Jesus asked the Twelve, 'Will you also go away?' ⁶⁸Peter answered him, 'Lord, to whom shall we go? You have the words of eternal life. ⁶⁹We have come to believe and now we know that you are the Holy One of God.'

⁷⁰Jesus said to them, 'I chose you, the Twelve, did I not? Yet one of you is a devil.' ⁷¹Jesus spoke of Judas Iscariot, the son of Simon. He, one of the Twelve, was to betray him.

As usual in this gospel, the reactions to Jesus are polarised into unbelief and belief. The unbelievers said that it was crazy talk, totally unacceptable. The same reaction is shared by people who reject belief in the Eucharist on the false understanding that it involves eating the physical flesh of Jesus. In 6:62 Jesus replies to this objection by appealing to them to keep their minds open until the time of his glorification. 'Does this offend you? Then how will you react when you see the Son of Man ascending to where he was before?' This reference to his future glorification is vital to an understanding of the Eucharist. It is the Risen Lord who is met under the signs of bread and wine. It does not involve eating physical flesh or drinking physical blood in a cannibalistic manner.

The grace to believe in the words of Jesus is a gift of the Holy Spirit. 'It is the spirit that gives life, the flesh cannot help. The words that I have spoken to you are spirit and they are life. Yet among you there are some who do not believe' (6:64).

Belief is a gift of the divine spirit: natural knowledge, or the flesh, does not bring faith. Scientific examination of the Eucharist is of no avail. Belief in the Eucharist has no foundation other than 'the words that I have spoken to you.' The words of Jesus are spirit as opposed to the flesh.

Those who did not believe turned their backs and no longer journeyed with Jesus. If Jesus did not intend his words to be taken in a literal sense, he should in all justice have called them back. 'Hey! Come back. You got me wrong. I did not mean it to be taken literally that I would give you my flesh to eat and my blood to drink.' But he had to let them go because he meant every word that he had spoken.

Some, however, stayed with him. Their spokesperson was Simon Peter who stated their belief in the words of Jesus. 'Lord, to whom shall we go? You have the words of eternal life. We have come to believe and now we know that you are the Holy One of God' (6:68-69).

The first mention of the betrayal of Judas is made here. Perhaps John is telling us that Judas began to turn from Jesus on the issue of giving his flesh to eat and his blood to drink. His final walking away from Jesus, into the dark of night, took place at the last supper, again at the time just before the Passover feast.

The deeds of Jesus when he fed the people miraculously and crossed the sea were signs of what he would do in the new Passover. In place of the manna of old, he would feed his people with eternal life through the wisdom of his word and with the meal of his glorified flesh and blood. This double feeding is the basis for the two tables in eucharistic liturgy, namely the table of the word and the table of the sacrificial banquet.

In crossing the Sea of Tiberias, Jesus recalled the exodus crossing of the Red Sea and foreshadowed the greatest journey of all in his return from this world to the Father. This lengthy chapter is a key development, one that divided his followers into unbelievers and true believers.

Praying

Lord, to whom shall we go. You have the words of eternal life. We believe, Lord, strengthen our faith.

Strengthen our faith as we grow in love of your holy words, as we chew them and draw life from them.

Strengthen our faith in your presence in the holy bread of Eucharist. May we become what we hear and receive. May we be one with you as you live in us and we live in you. Drawing life from you, may our thinking, our values, attitudes and behaviour increasingly manifest you to the world.

O Lord, we pray for those who have walked away from your holy table. Help them to hear your word with understanding. May they receive the gift of faith and be drawn to receive your holy presence.

You have the words of eternal life.

You are the Bread of Life.

John 7 & 8: Feast of Tabernacles

The seventh and eighth chapters of John form the most difficult section of any gospel. The tone is hostile and it is hard to keep track of the changing themes. There are misunderstandings and arguments about where Jesus has come from, where he is going to, his authority, his relationship with Abraham, about who are the true children of Abraham, and who is free or who is slave. The disjointed narrative captures the mood of rising tension between the Jewish authorities and Jesus. There are as many as ten references in these chapters to the Jews seeking to arrest or kill Jesus.

What holds everything in unity is the liturgical setting, the Feast of Tabernacles, mentioned in 7:2. After the feasts of Sabbath and Passover, this is the third of the Jewish feasts whose theme is expanded by Jesus. Tabernacles celebrated the faith of the Jews during the wandering years of the Exodus when they lacked the material security of land and house and drew their trust from their faith in the God who had led them out of slavery. The tent or temporary dwelling became the symbol of their faith and trust in God.

The feast was celebrated in September and incorporated the agricultural festival of thanksgiving for the grape harvest as well as the prayers for rain for the coming season. The rainy season is normally between October and March. The religious celebration highlighted four aspects of the Exodus story.

1. It was a journey from slavery to freedom.
2. The temporary tents symbolised a people on the move, lacking the security of a land of their own or permanent houses.

3. They were led by a cloud by day and a pillar of flame by night.

4. Their lives were saved on occasion by a flow of water from a rock.

These four themes of slavery, travelling from and to, light-darkness and water from the rock are woven into John's narrative. It is a tapestry of interwoven strands rather than a simple story.

Water in the desert

¹After this Jesus went around Galilee; he would not go about in Judea because the Jews wanted to kill him. ²Now the Jewish feast of the Tents was at hand. ³So the brothers of Jesus said to him, 'Don't stay here; go instead to Judea and let your disciples see the works you are doing. ⁴Anyone who wants to be known doesn't work secretly. Since you are able to do these things, show yourself to the world.'

⁵His brothers spoke like this because they didn't believe in him. ⁶Jesus said to them, 'My time has not yet come, but your time is always here.

⁷The world cannot hate you; but it hates me because I bear witness and I show that its deeds are evil. ⁸Go up to the feast! I am not going to this feast, because my time has not yet come.'

⁹Jesus spoke like this and remained in Galilee. ¹⁰But after his brothers had gone to the festival, he also went up, not publicly but in secret. ¹¹The Jews were looking for him at the festival and asked, 'Where is he?' ¹²There was a lot of talk about him among the people. Some said, 'He is a good man,' but others replied, 'No, he is misleading the people.' ¹³Yet for fear of the Jews no one spoke openly about him.

¹⁴When the festival was half over, Jesus went to the Temple and began to teach. ¹⁵The Jews marvelled and said, 'How is it that he speaks with so much learning when he has had no teacher?'

¹⁶And Jesus answered them, 'My teaching is not mine, but it comes from the One who sent me. ¹⁷Anyone who does the will of God shall know whether my teaching is from God or if I speak on my own authority.

¹⁸He who speaks on his own authority wishes to gain honour for himself. But he who wants to give glory to him who sent him is truthful and there is no reason to doubt him.'

¹⁹Moses gave you the Law, didn't he? But none of you keep the Law. Why, then, do you want to kill me?'

²⁰The people replied, 'You have a demon: who wants to kill you.' ²¹Jesus said to them, 'I performed a single deed, and you are all astounded by it. ²²But remember the circumcision ordered by Moses – actually it was not Moses but the ancestors who began this practice. You circumcise a man even on the sabbath, ²³and you would break the Law if you refused to do so because of the sabbath. How is it, then, that you are indignant with me because I healed the whole person on the sabbath? ²⁴Do not judge by appearances, but according to what is right.'

²⁵Some of the people of Jerusalem said, 'Is this not the man they want to kill? ²⁶And here he is speaking freely, and they don't say a word to him? Can it be that the rulers know that this is really the Christ? ²⁷Yet, we know where this man comes from; but when the Christ appears, no one will know where he comes from.'

²⁸So Jesus announced in a loud voice in the Temple court where he was teaching, 'You say that you know me and know where I come from! I have not come of myself; I was sent by the One who is true, and you don't know him. ²⁹I know him for I come from him and he sent me.'

³⁰They would have arrested him, but no one laid hands on him because his time has not yet come. ³¹Many people in the crowd, however, believed in him and said, 'When the Christ comes, will he give more signs than this man does?'

³²The Pharisees heard all these rumours among the people; so the Pharisees and chief priests sent officers of the temple to arrest him. ³³Jesus then said, 'I shall be with you a little longer; after that I shall to to him who sent me. ³⁴You will look for me and you will not find me. Where I am you cannot come.'

³⁵The Jews said to one another, 'Where does this man intend to go that we shall not find him? Will he go abroad to the Jews dispersed among the Greek nations and teach the Greeks also? ³⁶What does he mean when he says: 'You will look for me and not find me', and: 'Where I am going you cannot come?'

³⁷On the last and greatest day of the festival, Jesus stood up and proclaimed, 'If anyone is thirsty, let him come to me; ³⁸and let him who believes in me drink, for the Scripture says: Out of him shall flow rivers of living water.'

³⁹Jesus was referring to the Spirit which those who believe in him were to receive; the Spirit had not yet been given because Jesus had not yet entered into his Glory.

⁴⁰Many who had been listening to these words began to say, 'This is the Prophet.' ⁴¹Others said, 'This is the Christ.' But some wondered,

'Would the Christ come from Galilee? [42]Doesn't Scripture say that the Christ is a descendant of David and from Bethlehem?' [43]So the crowd was divided over him. [44]Some wanted to arrest him, but no one laid hands on him.
[45]The officers of the Temple went back to the chief priests who asked them, 'Why didn't you bring him?' [46]The officers answered, 'No one ever spoke like this man.' [47]The Pharisees then said, 'So you, too, have been led astray! [48]Have any of the rulers or any of the Pharisees believed in him? [49]Only these cursed people, who have no knowledge of the Law!'
[50]Yet one of them, Nicodemus, who had gone to Jesus earlier, spoke out, [51]'Does our law condemn a man without first hearing him and knowing the facts?' [52]They replied, 'Do you, too, come from Galilee? Look it up and see for yourself that no prophet is to come from Galilee.'

At the time of Jesus, the celebration of Tabernacles in Jerusalem lasted for eight days and featured ceremonies with water and light. Each day water was carried in solemn procession from the Pool of Siloam to the temple. The name Siloam means *sent* and the water in that pool spurted from a rockface after flowing through a marvellously constructed underground conduit for four hundred metres. Playing on the name, Jesus identified himself as the one who was sent by God (7:16). Early in the chapter, Jesus did not go up for the feast in the company of his relations. He would go only at the right time *(kairos)*, a time not dictated by family or human considerations but by the will of the Father who sent him.

When he arrives in Jerusalem and starts to teach, it sparks off a series of questions about where he has come from, where he got his learning and the authority he claims. The memory of healing the cripple on the Sabbath proves convincing to some but to others his claim to a unique relationship with the Father sounds blasphemous and deserving of the death sentence. They think they know where Jesus has come from. But the irony is that he has come from One beyond their experience. The Tabernacles theme of the Exodus journey is reaching a new meaning in this debate about where Jesus has come from and where he is going to.

On the last and greatest day of the feast, Jesus expanded on the theme of water. 'If anyone is thirsty let him come to me: and let him who believes in me drink, for the Scripture says: "Out of him shall flow rivers of living water"' (Jn 7:37-38). The evangelist explains that he was speaking of the outpouring of the Spirit which took place after his glorification.

The people were more divided than ever about Jesus. Arguments raged about his origin, hence about his authority to make the claims he did. Nicodemus made a reasonable appeal for a fair hearing according to the Law. But blind hatred shouted down this voice of reason.

Connecting

'If anyone is thirsty, let him come to me; and let him who believes in me drink, for Scripture says: "Out of him shall flow rivers of living water".' The evangelist adds the explanation that Jesus was referring forward to the outpouring of the Holy Spirit in the time of his glorification. In those later days what was foreshadowed by water at the Feast of Tabernacles would reach its fulfilment.

The evangelist is here drawing together the various aspects of the theme of water in previous chapters.

At the wedding at Cana the water for purification was changed into the wine of celebration at the uniting of heaven and earth. Nicodemus was told of the need for birth into supernatural life by water and the Holy Spirit. At the well in Samaria, thirst for water leads to up the satisfaction of life's inner thirsts through a relationship with Jesus. For the cripple at the pool, entering the water was the way to the Promised Land of health and freedom. Then in Chapter 6, a miraculous crossing of the sea links the miracle of the loaves and fishes with the Exodus story and the first Passover.

Now at the Feast of Tabernacles, Jesus draws together these various ideas about water and points ahead to the time of his glorification. It reminds us of John 6:62 where Jesus explains that what he is saying about eating his flesh and drinking his blood could not be understood until after his glorification. The streams of water and blood which issued from the open side of Jesus on the cross were to be a symbol of the outpouring of the Holy Spirit upon the world at the return of Jesus to the Father.

The church is sensitive to the immensely sacred symbolism of water. At the climax of the church's liturgy, the Easter Vigil, after the celebrations of light and word, water is blessed for the celebration or renewal of baptism. And in various blessings, water is used as a reminder of baptism and as a symbol of the sanctifying Spirit.

Praying

Lord Jesus, we hear you invite all who are thirsty to come to you. We experience thirst in many forms: thirst for meaning and direction; thirst for mercy and forgiveness; thirst for love and relationships; a deep thirst for what is lasting and eternal.

Once you provided water from a rock to save your people in the desert. Now you are the Rock from whom flows the waters of all satisfaction: fresh, living water pouring forth from your open heart.

Pour out your Spirit upon us, irrigating the seeds of divine life within us, flowering in lives of Christian virtue.

O God, you are my God, for you I long. For you my soul is thirsting.

John 8:1-11
> ¹As for Jesus, he went to the Mount of Olives.
> ²At daybreak Jesus appeared in the Temple again. All the people came to him, and he sat down and began to teach them.
> ³Then the teachers of the Law and the Pharisees brought in a woman who had been caught in the act of adultery. They made her stand in front of everyone. ⁴'Master,' they said, 'this woman has been caught in the act of adultery. ⁵Now the Law of Moses orders that such women be stoned to death; but you, what do you say?' ⁶They said this to test Jesus, so they could have some charges against him.
> Jesus bent down and started writing on the ground with his finger. ⁷And as they continued to ask him, he straightened up and said to them, 'Let the man among you who has no sin be the first to throw a

stone at her.' ⁸And he bent down again, writing on the ground.
⁹As a result of these words, they went away, one by one, starting with the oldest, and Jesus was left alone with the woman standing before him. ¹⁰Then Jesus straightened up and said to her, 'Woman, where are they? Has no one condemned you?' ¹¹She replied, 'No one.' And Jesus said, 'Neither do I condemn you; go away and don't sin again.'

The meeting of Jesus with the angry crowd and the woman arrested for adultery is one of the great stories of scripture, manifesting the mercy and wisdom of Jesus. Who can forget his challenge to our hypocrisy: 'Let whoever is without sin cast the first stone'? However, the vast majority of scholars are of the opinion that this story did not originally belong to this part of John's gospel as it interrupts the development of the Feast of Tabernacles. So, we will move on to the resumption of the debate at the feast in Jerusalem.

Light of the World

¹²Jesus spoke to them again, 'I am the Light of the world; he who follows me will not walk in darkness, but will have light and life.'
¹³The Pharisees replied, 'Now you are speaking on your own behalf, your testimony is worthless.'
¹⁴Then Jesus said, 'Even though I bear witness to myself, my testimony is true, for I know where I am going. But you do not know where I came from or where I am going.
¹⁵You judge by human standards; as for me I don't judge anyone.
¹⁶But if I had to judge, my judgement would be valid for I am not alone: the Father who sent me is with me. ¹⁷In your Law it is written that the testimony of two men is valid; ¹⁸so I am bearing witness to myself, and the Father who sent me bears witness to me.'
¹⁹They asked him, 'Where is your Father?' Jesus answered, 'You don't know me or my Father; if you knew me, you would know my Father as well.'
²⁰Jesus said these things when he was teaching in the Temple area, in the place where they received the offerings. Yet no one arrested him, because his hour had not yet come.
²¹Again Jesus said to them, 'I am going away, and though you look for me, you will die in your sin. Where I am going you cannot come.' ²²The Jews wondered, 'Why does he say that we can't come where he is going? Will he kill himself?'

23But Jesus said, 'You are from below and I am from above; you are of this world and I am not of this world. 24This is why I told you that you will die in your sins. And you shall die in your sins unless you believe that I am He.'
25They asked him, 'Who are you?', and Jesus said, 'Just what I have told you from the beginning. 26I have much to say about you and much to condemn; but the One who sent me is truthful and everything I learned from him, I proclaim to the world.'
27They didn't understand that Jesus was speaking to them about the Father. 28So Jesus said, 'When you have lifted up the Son of Man, then you will know that I am He and that I do nothing of myself, but I speak just as the Father taught me. 29He who sent me is with me and has not left me alone; indeed, I always do what please him.'
30As Jesus spoke like this, many believed in him. 31Jesus went on to say to the Jews who believed in him: 'You will be my true disciples if you keep my word. 32Then you will know the truth and the truth will make you free.' 33They answered him, 'We are the descendants of Abraham and have never been slaves of anyone. What do you mean by saying: You will be free?'
34Jesus answered them, 'Truly, I say to you, whoever commits sin is a slave. 35But the slave doesn't stay in the house forever. 36So, if the Son makes you free, you will be really free.
37I know that you are the descendants of Abraham; yet you want to kill me because my word finds no place in you. 38So, while I speak of what I have seen in the Father's presence, you do what you have learned from your father.'
39They answered him, 'Our father is Abraham.' Then Jesus said, 'If you were Abraham's children, you would do as Abraham did. 40You want to kill me because I am the one who tells you the truth – the truth that I have learned from God. That is not what Abraham did; 41but you are doing the works of your father.'
The Jews said to him, 'We are not illegitimate children; we have one Father, God.' 42Jesus replied, 'If God were your Father you would love me, for I came forth from God, and I am here. And I didn't come by my own decision, but it was he himself who sent me. 43Why do you not understand my teaching? It is because you cannot bear my message.
44The father you spring from is the devil and you will carry out the evil wishes of your father, who has been a murderer from the beginning. He didn't uphold the truth for, in him, there is no truth; and now, when he speaks for himself, he lies. He is a liar and the father of lies.

⁴⁵Now I tell the truth and you don't believe me. ⁴⁶Which of you could find something false in me? Then, if I am telling the truth, why do you not believe me? ⁴⁷He who is God hears the words of God; you don't hear because you are not God.'
⁴⁸The Jews retorted, 'So we are right in saying that you are a Samaritan and are possessed by a demon.' ⁴⁹Jesus said, 'I am not possessed, and you try to shame me when I give honour to my Father. ⁵⁰I don't care about my own glory; there is One who cares for me and he will be the judge.
⁵¹Truly, I say to you, if anyone keeps my word he will never experience death.' ⁵²The Jews replied, 'Now we know that you have a demon. Abraham died and the prophets as well, but you say: "Whoever keeps my word will never experience death." Who do you claim to be? ⁵³Do you claim to be greater than our father Abraham, who died? And the prophets also died.'
⁵⁴Then Jesus said, 'If I would praise myself, it would count for nothing. But he who gives glory to me is the Father, the very One you claim as your God, ⁵⁵although you don't him. I know him and if I were to say that I don't know him, I would be a liar like you. But, I know him and I keep his word.
⁵⁶As for Abraham, your ancestor, he looked forward to the day when I could come; and he rejoiced when he saw it.'
⁵⁷The Jews then said to him, 'You are not yet fifty years old and you have seen Abraham?' ⁵⁸And Jesus said, 'Truly, I say to you, before Abraham was, I am.' ⁵⁹They then picked up stones to throw at him, but Jesus hid himself and left the Temple.

The celebration of Tabernacles featured a brilliant torchlight procession in the Women's Court of the Temple to recall the lights which led the people during the Exodus. As he had replaced the ceremonial water with the promise of the outpouring of the Spirit, Jesus now proclaims that he is the Light of the world. 'I am the Light of the world; he who follows me will not walk in the darkness, but will have light and life' (8:12).

A heated debate with the Pharisees follows. They argue about the validity of the testimony of Jesus on his own behalf. There is confusion about where Jesus came from and where he is going to. The journey of Jesus will finally lead to his return to the Father, the ultimate event which was foreshadowed by the Exodus journey from slavery to freedom.

Since they failed to understand that he was talking about the Father (8:27), Jesus again refers forward to the time of his glorification: 'When you have lifted up the Son of Man, then you will know that I am He and that I do nothing of myself, but I say just what the Father taught me' (8:28). We have already met two instances when Jesus explained that what he was saying about the Bread of Life (6:62) and the outpouring of the Spirit (7:39) would be understood only in the light of his return to the Father.

As usual in this gospel, the Jews are divided into unbelievers and believers. To the Jews who believed in him Jesus said: 'If you remain in my word you will be my true disciples: and you will know the truth and the truth will set you free' (8:31-32). The Feast of Tabernacles was about impermanent dwellings. Now Jesus is proclaiming that belief in his word will build that permanent home which offers truth and freedom.

Mention of freedom, the great fruit of the Exodus, sparked the Pharisees into defending their freedom as descendants of Abraham. But Jesus replied that true children of Abraham would do as he did, namely, believe the word of God. And that word was now coming to them in the truth that he was bringing them. The way they were behaving showed them up as children of the devil who was a murderer from the beginning and the father of lies. Then, as to his own identity Jesus made an awesome assertion, 'Truly, I say to you, before Abraham was, I am.' Because this claim echoed the divine name revealed to Moses, it was taken as blasphemy, so they picked up stones to throw at him.

Connecting

We connect with the story by reflecting on the faith which was celebrated at the Feast of Tabernacles and on our own experiences in the pilgrimage of life as followers of the light of Jesus.

Religious Jews to this day erect temporary dwellings, open to natural light and the prevailing elements, for this feast. Rabbi Jonathan Sacks recalls how on one particularly stormy night his own rather flimsy construction was held in place by a single nail while his friend's masterpiece of carpentry floundered in the gale. He saw the nail as a symbol of faith. 'The tabernacle in all its vulnerability symbolises faith: the faith of a people who set out long ago on a risk-laden journey across a desert of space and time with no more protection than the sheltering divine presence ... To know that life is full of risk and yet to affirm it, to sense the full insecurity of the human situation and yet to rejoice: this, for me, is the essence of faith. Judaism is no comforting illusion that all is well in this dark world. It is instead the courage to celebrate in the midst of uncertainty and to rejoice even in the transitory shelter of the tabernacle, the Jewish symbol of faith' (Sacks: *Faith in the Future*, DLT, 1995, 150f.).

At the celebration of the feast in the Jerusalem temple Jesus declared: 'I am the Light of the world: he who follows me will not walk in darkness, but will have light and life' (8:12). And he told his disciples to make their home in his word.

Faith in Jesus gives us light about divine creation and the eternal destiny of life. It is the good news of salvation from sin. It gives us the moral light on how we ought to live. It brings the light of God's face in the consolations of prayer. It is the pillar of light through the darkness of night.

But faith is also the cloud of darkness which covers the mysterious ways of God which remain beyond the reach of human knowing. How can a loving God permit human suffering? The death of the mother of a young family? That good people have to endure misfortune and often the shady character appears to prosper? Faith is not a simplistic assertion that there are no mysteries beyond our understanding. Not everything is clear.

Reflecting on Simeon's prophecy about the rejection of Jesus and the sword of sorrow which Mary would endure, Pope John Paul wrote that Mary conformed herself to God's mysterious plans in 'the dim light of faith'. The pilgrimage of faith is with the light of certainty, yet in the dimness of obscurity: a pillar of light by night and a cloud by day.

The Catechism of the Catholic Church, 157, makes an important assertion that faith can be certain and obscure at the same time.

'Faith is certain. It is more certain than all human knowledge because it is founded on the very word of God who cannot lie. Yet, revealed truths can be obscure to human reason and experience, but the certainty that the divine light gives is greater than the light which natural reason gives.' The famous response of Cardinal Newman is then quoted: 'Ten thousand difficulties do not make one doubt.'

Growth in faith resembles emotional growth through the stages of childhood, adolescence and adulthood. Child faith is characterised by a blind, unquestioning acceptance of what others say. Adolescent faith seeks independence. God is accepted as friend on more or less equal terms but there may be big problems with the mystery and authority of God. Adult faith accepts the mystery of God beyond one's understanding, yet it has reached unshakeable certainty.

How do the terms *certain* and *obscure* apply to the three stages?

Child faith is certain but it has no room for obscurities.

Adolescent faith is quite uncertain and obscure.

Adult faith has attained certainty while it has room for the obscure.

Those who adopt a fundamentalist approach to scripture usually fall into the category of child faith. They are absolutely certain that their reading of a text is the correct one. They can see no other possible interpretation or engage in reasonable argument. Sometimes they employ a very convenient way of dismissing whatever does not fit into their system by saying that it is from the devil. This can mean dismissing psychological systems, self-development practices, alternative medicine or systems of meditation on the grounds that they are not mentioned in the bible.

The American writer, Flannery O'Connor, wrote a book called *Death of a Child* on the short life and great faith of Mary Ann Long who died aged twelve. During her final illness, an enthusiastic evangelical approached Mary Ann: 'The Lord Jesus can heal you!' Her weak voice replied: 'I know he can heal me. I know he can do anything. It doesn't make a bit of difference whether he heals me or not. That's his business.' What did the man do? 'He looked at me funny-like and then went away.'

Though a child in years, Mary Ann's pilgrimage through the crucible of suffering had developed in her an adult faith. She was calmly certain about God and willing to accept the mysteries beyond comprehension.

The Feast of Tabernacles celebrated the faith of the desert pilgrims through light and darkness, certainty and obscurity. At that feast Jesus took the water and promised the outpouring of the Holy Spirit who would be an unending source of living water in the heart of the believer. And he called himself the Light of the world. 'He who follows me will not walk in darkness, but will have light and life.'

Praying

Lord Jesus, you are the light of the world. If we follow you we will not be walking in the dark. In your light we see light.

Yet as we journey through our Exodus of life we sometimes struggle with what we cannot understand. Sometimes the ways of providence are incomprehensible to us and hard to accept. Our journey is through night and day, darkness and light, obscurity and certainty.

Much of the confusion of life is caused by the devil who is the father of lies and a murderer from the beginning.

But our strength is in your word.

You invite us to make our home in your word.

There you promise us truth, a truth that will make us free, a truth that will silence the foe.

Lord Jesus, lifted up from the earth in the mystery of the cross and the light of your glorification, draw us to you.

Your word is a lamp for our steps and a light for our way.

John 9:1-41: Light for the Blind

¹As Jesus walked along, he saw a man who had been blind from birth. ²His disciples asked him, 'Master, if he was born blind because of sin, was it his sin or his parents?' ³Jesus answered, 'Neither this man nor his parents sinned; he was born blind so that God's power might be shown in him. ⁴While it is day we must do the work of the One who sent me; for the night will come when no one can work. ⁵As long as I am in the world, I am the light of the world.'
⁶As Jesus said this, he made paste with spittle and clay and rubbed it on the eyes of the blind man. ⁷Then, he told him, 'Go and wash in the Pool of Siloam.' (This name means sent). So he went and washed and came back able to see.
⁸His neighbours and all the people who used to see him begging, wondered. They said, 'Is this not the beggar who used to sit here?' ⁹Some said, 'It's he;' Others said, 'No, but he looks like him.' But the man himself said, 'I am the one.' ¹⁰Then they asked, 'How is it that your eyes were opened?' ¹¹And he answered, 'The man called Jesus made a mud paste, put it on my eyes and said to me: 'Go to Siloam and wash.' So I went, and washed, and I could see.' ¹²They asked, 'Where is he?' and the man answered, 'I don't know.'
¹³Now it was a sabbath day when Jesus made mud paste and opened the eyes of the blind man. ¹⁴The people brought the man to the Pharisees ¹⁵who asked him again, 'How did you recover your sight?' And he said once more, 'He put paste on my eyes, and I washed and now I see.' ¹⁶Some of the Pharisees said, 'This man is not from God, for he works on the sabbath'; but others wondered, 'How can a sinner perform such miraculous signs?' So they were divided ¹⁷and they questioned the blind man again, 'What do you think of this man who opened your eyes?' And he answered, 'He is a prophet.'
¹⁸After all this, the Jews refused to believe that the man had been

blind and had recovered his sight; so they called his parents [19]and asked them, 'Is this your son? You say that he was born blind, how is it that he now sees?' [20]The parents answered, 'He really is our son and he was born blind; [21]but how it is that he now sees, we don't know, neither do we know who opened his eyes. Ask him, he is old enough. Let him speak for himself.'

[22]The parents said this because they feared the Jews who had already agreed that whoever confessed Jesus to be the Christ was to be put out of the Jewish community. [23]Because of this his parents said, 'He is old enough, ask him.'

[24]So a second time the Pharisees called the man who had been blind, and they said to him, 'Tell us the truth; we know that this man is a sinner.' [25]He replied, 'I don't know whether he is a sinner or not; I only know that I was blind and now I see.' [26]They said to him, 'What did he do to you? How did he open your eyes?' [27]He replied, 'I have told you already and you would not listen. Why do you want to hear it again? Do you also want to become his disciples?'

[28]Then they started to insult him. 'Become his disciple yourself! We are disciples of Moses. [29]We know that God has spoken to Moses, but as for this man we don't know where he comes from.'

[30]The man replied, 'It is amazing that you don't know where the man comes from, and yet he opened my eyes!

[31]We know that God doesn't listen to sinners, but if anyone honours God and does his will, God listens to him. [32]Never, since the world began, has it been heard that anyone opened the eyes of a person who was born blind. [33]If this man were not from God, he could do nothing.'

[34]They answered him, 'You were born a sinner and now you teach us!' And they drove him away.

[35]Jesus heard that they had driven him away. He found him and said, 'Do you believe in the Son of Man?' [36]He answered, 'Who is he, that I may believe in him?' [37]Jesus said, 'You have seen him and he is speaking to you.' [38]The man said, 'Lord, I believe', and worshipped him. [39]Jesus said: 'I came into this world to carry out a judgement: Those who do not see shall see, and those who see shall become blind.' [40]Some Pharisees stood by and asked him, 'So we are blind?' [41]And Jesus answered, 'If you were blind, you would not be guilty. Now that you say: "We see", this is the proof of your sin.'

The healing of the man who was born blind is set within the context of the Feast of Tabernacles. The miracle is a sign which verifies the claim of Jesus made during the celebration of the feast: 'I am the light of the world' (Jn 8:12).

The great themes of Tabernacles, which we have previously noted, recur in this story. The journey theme is announced in the opening verse as Jesus is portrayed as walking along. Tabernacles recalled the lights which led the Exodus: Jesus says, 'As long as I am in the world, I am the light of the world' (9:5). The water from the rock is recalled as Jesus sends the man to wash in the Pool of Siloam where the water has been sent through the underground tunnel. The Exodus escape from slavery is celebrated in the escape of the man from blindness. By contrast, the Pharisees are left in the blindness of rejection.

As in the story of the woman at the well and the cripple at the pool, this man here is not named by the evangelist. It invites the reader to see him as more than an individual. He represents stages in development of faith.

His story is taken up from the very beginning for we are told that he was blind from birth. At this point we meet the simplistic certainty of the fundamentalist who asserts that this blindness was caused by sin, either on the part of his parents or through his own sins. How he might have sinned before birth they do not explain! Jesus dismissed their assumption and placed the blindness in the greater context of God's mysterious works. As we saw in the last chapter, mature faith finds room for the obscurities of God's designs.

Early in the story the man exhibits the finer qualities of childhood in his unquestioning obedience and trust when Jesus sends him to Siloam. There is a childlike innocence in the way he repeats his explanation of what happened: 'I went, I washed and I could see.'

As the story progresses, his maturity and independence develop. His parents testify that he is old enough to speak for himself. At his second interrogation he shows courage and an independent mind. He distinguishes between what he does not know (whether Jesus was a sinner) and what he does know (that he was blind once but now can see). Furthermore, he argues with mature logic. When the Jews go back to the authority of Moses regarding Sabbath observance, he goes back to the older authority of the Creation narrative: 'Never, since the world began, has it been heard that anyone opened the eyes of a person who was born blind. If this man were not from God, he could do nothing' (9:32-33).

His growth in faith reaches full maturity when Jesus identifies himself as the Son of Man. At this the man said 'Lord, I believe,' and he worshipped him.

Connecting

In the last chapter we quoted *The Catechism of the Catholic Church*, par. 157, about the certainty and obscurity of faith. The following paragraph, 158, is about the development of faith. 'Faith seeks understanding: it is intrinsic to faith that the believer desires to know better the One in whom he has put his faith and to understand better what he has revealed; a more penetrating knowledge will in turn call forth a greater faith, increasingly set afire by love ...'

The story of this man's development is a model of growth in faith. Like the Samaritan woman, this man shows his growth in faith by the rising dignity of the way that he refers to Jesus. Initially, he refers to him as 'the man called Jesus'. Later, when asked what did he think of Jesus, he answered, 'He is a prophet.' By the end of the story, the title he gives to Jesus is Lord.

These titles of ascending recognition express the believer's growth in faith. Beginning with Jesus the man, one admires his human qualities. He sets an example to follow. If one wants to know what God is like, the surest starting point is to study the life of Jesus. Jesus on earth was the Word of God expressed in the language of human life. The gospels are our primary source for the knowledge of Jesus. Ignorance of the scriptures is ignorance of Christ, as Saint Jerome remarked. The journey of Christian faith begins in learning about Jesus.

But admiration of Jesus is only the beginning of a faith-relationship. The teaching of Jesus is more taken to heart in recognising him as a prophet or revealer of the divine. The mind is increasingly enlightened by the teaching of Christ and his value system is absorbed into one's practical decisions. Saint Paul called it putting on the mind of Christ. From this will flow patterns of Christlike attitudes, values and behaviour. 'You were once darkness, but now you are light in the Lord. Behave as children of light; the fruits of light are kindness, justice and truth in every form' (Eph 5:8-9).

Faith develops from admiration of Jesus in his humanity, through the reflection of his light in practical action and then reaches a total acceptance of the Lordship of Christ. The man in the story was given the revelation of Jesus as Lord. When he uses this title he bows in humble worship. One makes a total submission of intellect and will to the Lord, handing over the past to his mercy, the present to his direction and the future to his providence.

In the early church, baptism was sometimes known as enlightenment. The story of the journey of the man from blindness to the light of worship has been associated with baptism since the earliest days. Drawings on the walls of the underground catacombs in Rome bear historical testimony. The story is still used in the journey of a catechumen towards the sacrament of baptism.

Prayer

Father of mercy, you helped the man born blind to believe in your Son and through that faith to reach the light of your Kingdom.

Free us from the falsehoods that surround and blind us.

Let truth be the foundation of our lives.

May we live in your light forever.

Lord Jesus, you are the true light that enlightens all people.

In the breath of the Holy Spirit fan into flame the goodwill of all who have received your light in baptism.

May our eyes be fixed on you as the light of life and the model of all virtue.

May our minds be enlightened by your teaching and our values be according to your kingdom.

John 10:1-21: The Good Shepherd

¹Truly, I say to you, he who does not enter the sheepfold by the gate, but climbs in some other way, is a thief and a robber. ²But the shepherd of the sheep enters by the gate. ³The keeper opens the gate to him and the sheep hear his voice; he calls each of his sheep by name and leads them out. ⁴When he has brought out all his own, he goes before them and the sheep follow him for they know his voice. ⁵A stranger they will not follow, rather they will run away from him because they don't recognise a stranger's voice.'
⁶Jesus used this comparison, but they did not understand what he was saying to them.
⁷So Jesus said, 'Truly, I say to you, I am the shepherd of the sheep. ⁸All who came were thieves and robbers, and the sheep did not hear them. ⁹I am the gate. Whoever enters through me will be saved; he will go in and out freely and find food.
¹⁰The thief comes to steal and kill and destroy, but I have come that they may have life, life in all its fullness.
¹¹I am the good shepherd. The good shepherd gives his life for the sheep. ¹²Not so the hired man or any other person who is not the shepherd and to whom the sheep do not belong. He abandons the sheep as soon as he sees the wolf coming; then the wolf snatches and scatters the sheep. ¹³He is only a hired man and he cares nothing for the sheep.
¹⁴I am the good shepherd, I know my own and my own know me, ¹⁵as the Father knows me and I know the Father. Because of this I give my life for the sheep.
¹⁶I have other sheep that are not of this fold. These I have to lead as well, and they shall listen to my voice. Then there will be one flock since there is one Shepherd.
¹⁷The Father loves me because I lay down my life so as to take it up again. ¹⁸No one takes it from me, but I lay down freely. It is mine to lay down and to take up again: this mission I received from my Father.'
¹⁹Because of these words, the Jews were divided again. ²⁰Many of

them said, 'He has a demon and is out of his mind. Why listen to him?' [21]But others said, 'A possessed man doesn't speak in this way. Can a demon open the eyes of the blind?'

After the arguments and tension of the last three chapters it is refreshing to meet the attractive figure of the Good Shepherd. In the synoptic gospels Jesus is the shepherd who feeds the people with his teaching and shows his care by seeking out the lost sheep. Here in John's gospel the emphasis is on the self-sacrificing devotion of Jesus in contrast to those religious leaders who used their position to have power and to feather their own nests. Jesus called himself the good or true shepherd in contrast to these false leaders.

As usual in this gospel, the liturgical context is important. The Feast of Dedication will be mentioned in John 10:22. Each year, during the celebration of this feast, the words of Ezechiel about the shepherds of Israel were read aloud. 'Son of Man, speak on my behalf against the shepherds of Israel! Woe to the shepherds of Israel who feed themselves! Should not the shepherds feed the flock?' (Ezec 34:2). Ezechiel complained that these self-seeking leaders had allowed the flock to be scattered but God would send a true shepherd who would gather back the strays into one flock. Jesus identified himself as that true shepherd.

In contrast to the careless shepherds, Jesus emphasised three positive qualities of his own pastoral care:
- he lays down his life for the sheep;
- he knows his sheep and is known by them;
- he gathers them into the one flock.

Connecting

'I am the gate. Whoever enters through me will be saved; he will go in and out freely and find food' (10:9).

Usually there was no gate as such in the sheep-pen. The shepherd stayed there and acted as the gate. Jesus is the only Saviour, the only way to heaven. There is no other name by which one can attain eternal salvation. His love for us was shown especially when he laid down his life and shed his blood for the remission of sins.

The shepherd acting as the gate is there to keep out dangerous intruders. Jesus is our protection. His support and strength are available to us. The sacraments are ritual celebrations of his constant support at all the vital times of life – birth, adolescence, marriage, illness, divine food for the daily pilgrimage of life and forgiveness of sin.

He encourages us to knock on his door, to ask his help and to seek his presence. Jesus is the gate that opens up eternal life to us: the gate who protects us from harm.

'I have come that they may have life, life in all its fullness' (10:10).

What is this fullness of life? Today there are false shepherds who misinterpret these words in the sense of material blessings. Many of the television preachers proclaim a prosperity gospel. Hand your life over to Jesus, be converted to a good life and then your business will prosper and your health flourish. This was an Old Testament idea of blessedness dating from a time before the people had a belief in life after death. In the Sermon on the Mount Jesus reversed many of the old, imperfect concepts. In his eyes, the blessed are those who lack the prosperity, power, prestige and popularity that went with the old idea of blessing. The blessed ones of Jesus' vision belong here and now to his kingdom but their rewards and satisfaction are not seen until the future. Today's prosperity gospel, or Cadillac Christianity as it is also called, is a contradiction of the teaching of Jesus.

What, then, is this fullness of life that Jesus promised? In terms of time, he offers a life that extends beyond death: a life that never ends.

And what he offers is a life that brings fullness of growth in virtue. Human beings were made in the image and likeness of God. But sin gets a grip on us and blots out the reflection of God in our lives. Traces of selfishness, anger, envy, lust, pride and so on cloud over the light of God's image. But Jesus is the caring Shepherd who seeks out the lost. Near restful waters he leads us to revive our drooping spirits. 'My head you have anointed with oil ...' The Good Shepherd heals the lacerations and scratches of life.

If we take the Christian life seriously and co-operate with the grace of God, then we will grow in the virtues of love, hope, patience, kindness, forgiveness, courage and all other strengths of the noble character. The grace of God restores people to being what they were originally meant to be, images or reflections of God.

Saint Irenaeus had a famous saying that the glory of God is seen in a person who is fully alive. And to be fully alive, he says, is to have one's face turned to God, catching the light and love of God, reflecting God into the world. In fact, the fullness that Jesus offers is nothing less than a participation in divine life. 'It is no longer I who live, but Christ lives in me' (Gal 2:20).

'I know my own and my own know me, as the Father knows me and I know the Father' (10:14).

The shepherds of Jesus' time lived for months on end with the sheep and had pet names on each one. The sheep on their part knew the shepherd and responded to his calls and whistles.

It is extraordinary to think that of all the millions of people on this earth, God knows each one of us with a special, individual love. Think of any big city and the teeming throngs on streets and trains. Yet each one is unique and important to God. Furthermore, God wants us to know that we are known by him. God desires that we would grow in our knowledge of his love. This sort of knowing belongs to love and resides in the heart. In some languages, to know somebody could mean having an intimate encounter.

To know God as one is known by God is at the heart of contemplative prayer. Saint Teresa of Avila called it 'a close sharing between friends; it means taking time frequently to be alone with him who we know loves us.' The soul constantly seeks the beloved with intense desire. Constant attentiveness to God becomes the focus of the mind and the desire of the heart.

The new Catechism stresses the need for a determined will to make time for God. 'One does not undertake contemplative prayer only when one has the time: one makes time for the Lord, with the firm determination not to give up, no matter what trials and darkness one may encounter. One cannot always meditate, but one can always enter into inner prayer, independently of the conditions of health, work or emotional state. The heart is the place of the quest and encounter, in poverty and faith' (CCC 2710).

Jesus, the Good Shepherd freely embraced the poverty of laying down his life for his beloved. Responding to him demands the poverty of emptying one's life of materialistic preoccupation and sensual pursuits. Like Jesus, one is given over to seeking always the will of the Father

Jesus raised the discourse on the Good Shepherd to the level of his relationship with the Father. His love for the Father would be manifested by laying down his life in obedience to the mission given him by the Father. Similarly, the person who advances in loving intimacy with Jesus makes the Father's will the supreme desire of life.

Praying

Lord Jesus, you are our shepherd, there is nothing we shall want.

You, the Gate, open up for us the way to fullness of life, even a sharing in divine life.

To the restful waters of prayer you lead us to revive our drooping spirits. There you call us to spend time with you, knowing you as we are known by you.

When we walk in the valley of darkness you are there. And your cross tells us that you love us unto the laying down of your life for us. So we shall not fear.

Good Shepherd, call back the strays and gather all into the one family of God.

As we follow you, Good Shepherd, surely goodness and kindness will surround us all the days of our lives.

John 10:22-39: The Feast of Dedication

The Consecrated One

22 The time came for the feast of the Dedication. It was winter 23 and Jesus walked back and forth in the portico of Solomon. 24 The Jews then gathered around him and said to him, 'How long will you keep us in doubt? If you are the Messiah, tell us plainly.' 25 Jesus answered, 'I have already told you but you do not believe. 26 The works I do in my Father's name proclaim who I am, but you don't believe because, as I said, you are not my sheep.

27 My sheep hear my voice and I know them; they follow me 28 and I give them eternal life. They shall never perish and no one will ever steal them from me. 29 What the Father has given me is stronger than everything and no one can snatch it from the Father's hand. 30 I and the Father are one.'

31 The Jews then picked up stones to throw at him; 32 so Jesus said, 'I have openly done many good works among you which the Father gave me to do. For which of these do you stone me?'

33 The Jews answered, 'We are not stoning you for doing good work but for insulting God; you are only a man and you make yourself God.'

34 Then Jesus replied, 'Is this not written in your Law: I said: you are gods? 35 So those who received the word of God were called gods and the Scripture is always true. 36 Then what should be said of the one anointed and sent into the world by the Father? Am I insulting God when I say: "I am the Son of God"?

37 If I am not doing the works of my Father, do not believe me. 38 But if I do them, even though you don't put faith in me, believe me because of the works I do, and know that the Father is in me and I in the Father.'

39 Again they tried to arrest him, but Jesus escaped from their hands.

The fourth Jewish festival to receive a fuller meaning from Jesus was the Feast of Dedication. This was a relatively recent feast, established in 163BC, at the time of the Maccabees, to celebrate the rededication of the temple after it had been profaned two years previously by Greek statues and pagan worship.

As the gospel notes, it was a mid-winter feast, commencing on the twenty-fifth day of Kisleau (roughly our December) and running for eight days. Each day there was a procession with lights and branches, two appropriate symbols of the prospect of spring now that the passing of mid-winter had reversed the shortening of the days.

In the fourth century of the Christian era, in an effort to counteract the pagan feast of the returning sun, the church promoted the celebration of the birth of Jesus as the light of the world. The octave of Christmas begins of course on the twenty-fifth day of December and runs up to the first day of the new year.

The Feast of Dedication celebrated the consecration of the temple. Already in this gospel, Jesus has spoken about the destruction of that temple and of its replacement by his risen body as the sacred place of worship of the Father. Now he refers to himself as one who has been anointed or consecrated by the Father (10:36). And he makes two clear assertions of his unity with the Father. 'I and the Father are one' (10:30); 'The Father is in me and I in the Father' (10:38). So, the Feast of the Dedication is the occasion for Jesus to assert that he is the consecrated one sent by the Father. The name of Christ literally means the one who has been anointed.

Connecting

The union of Jesus and the Father is reflected in the union of Jesus with his flock. People who hear the voice of the Lord and faithfully follow him grow in intimate knowledge of God and enter eternal life. Not only is Jesus the consecrated one of God but his followers are consecrated in his name. The new temple of God's presence on earth is seen in the living stones of Christ's church on earth.

Saint Paul in his letters was very enthusiastic about the idea of the church being the new temple of God. Not only the church as a whole but he thought of the body of the individual Christian as a temple of the Holy Spirit. 'Do you not know that you are

JOHN 10:22-39: THE FEAST OF DEDICATION

God's temple, and that God's Spirit is within you? If anyone destroys this temple of God, God will destroy him. God's temple is holy, and you are that temple' (1 Cor 3:16-17).

Perhaps Paul's sense of the sacredness of the Christian's body is linked with his conversion experience. When he was on the road to hunt down followers of Jesus he heard the voice asking him, 'Saul, Saul, why do you persecute me?' When he asked, 'Who are you, Lord?', the voice told him, 'I am Jesus whom you are persecuting' (Acts 9:4-5). His sharp mind immediately understood what the risen Lord was saying to him: to touch the Christian was to touch the Lord himself. This meant that the baptised follower of Christ was united with the Lord. The beautiful name *Christian* expresses the consecration of the follower of Christ's way.

In the sacraments of baptism and confirmation the oil of chrism is used to anoint the body. Just as the sacred name of Christ means the anointed one of God, so too a chrismed Christian is an anointed temple of God's presence on earth.

Paul told the people of Corinth, a city where pagan temples were notorious for sexual licence, to consider their bodies as temples of God. 'Do you not know that your body is a temple of the Holy Spirit within you, given by God? You belong no longer to yourselves. Remember at what price you have been bought and make your bodies serve the glory of God' (1 Cor 6:19).

Through the sacred anointing of chrism, my body is a consecrated temple of God. My outer senses of sight, hearing, touch, smell and taste are consecrated to take in the rays of God's presence in the world. My inner senses, especially memory and imagination, are the great connecting powers which associate my daily experiences with the treasures of the past and the possibilities of the future.

Praying

Lord Jesus, you are the Christ, the anointed of the Father, the new temple.

You are ever totally dedicated to the will of the Father, one with the Father.

And you are the Good Shepherd who dedicated your very life to the flock.

The chrism of baptism and confirmation expresses the dedication of our lives to you. We are privileged to bear the name of Christian.

May we be true to what we are called.

May we be dedicated in mind to your way of thinking: dedicated in heart to your love: and dedicated in body to your service.

May we be living temples of the Father's glory, emptied of sin and filled with the Holy Spirit.

John 10:40-11:44: Raising of Lazarus

10 ⁴⁰He went away again to the other side of the Jordan, to the place where John had baptised, and there he stayed. ⁴¹Many people came to him and said, 'John showed no miraculous signs, but he spoke of this man and everything he said was true.' ⁴²And many became believers in that place.

11 ¹There was a sick man named Lazarus who was from Bethany, the village of Mary and her sister Martha. ²(It was the same Mary who anointed the Lord with perfume and wiped his feet with her hair.) Their brother Lazarus was sick. ³So the sisters sent this message to Jesus, 'Lord, the one you love is sick.' ⁴On hearing this Jesus said, 'This illness will not end in death; rather it is for God's glory and the Son of God will be glorified through it.' ⁵It is a fact that Jesus loved Martha and her sister and Lazarus; ⁶yet, after he heard of the illness of Lazarus, he stayed two days longer in the place where he was. ⁷Only then did he say to his disciples, 'Let us go into Judea again.' ⁸They replied, 'Master, recently the Jews wanted to stone you. Are you going there again?' ⁹Jesus said to them, 'Shall I not walk during the twelve hours of the day? Whoever walks in the daytime shall not stumble, for he sees with the light of the world. ¹⁰But if anyone walks by night, he will stumble for there is no light in him.' ¹¹After that Jesus said to them, 'Our friend Lazarus has fallen asleep, but I am going to wake him.' ¹²The disciples replied, 'Lord, a sick man who sleeps will recover.' ¹³But, Jesus had referred to Lazarus' death, and they thought that he had meant the repose of sleep. ¹⁴So Jesus said plainly, 'Lazarus is dead ¹⁵and for your sake I am glad I was not there, for now you may believe.' ¹⁶Then Thomas called the Twin said to his fellow disciples, 'Let us also go that we may die with him.'

¹⁷When Jesus came, he found that Lazarus had been in the tomb for four days. ¹⁸As Bethany is near Jerusalem, about two miles away, ¹⁹many Jews had come to Martha and Mary to offer consolation at their brother's death.

[20]When Martha heard that Jesus was coming, she went to meet him while Mary remained sitting in the house. [21]And she said to Jesus, 'Lord if you had been here, my brother would not have died. [22]But I know that whatever you ask from God, God will give you.' [23]Jesus said, 'Your brother will rise again.'
[24]Martha replied, 'I know that he will rise in the resurrection of the dead, at the last day.' [25]But Jesus said to her, I am the resurrection; whoever believes in me, though he die, shall live. [26]Whoever is alive by believing in me will never die. Do you believe this?'
[27]Martha then answered, 'Yes, Lord I have come to believe that you are the Christ, the Son of God, he who is coming into the world.'
[28]After that Martha went and called her sister Mary, quietly, saying, 'The Master is here and is calling for you.' [29]As soon as Mary heard this, she rose and went to him. [30]Jesus had not yet come into the village, but was still in the place where Martha had met him.
[31]The Jews who were with her in the house consoling her, also came. When they saw her get up and go out, they followed her, thinking that she was going to the tomb to weep.
[32]As for Mary, when she came to the place where Jesus was and saw him, she fell at his feet and said, [33]'Lord, if you had been there, my brother would not have died.' When Jesus saw her weeping and the Jews also who had come with her, he was moved in the depths of his spirit and troubled. [34]Then he asked, 'Where have you laid him?' They answered, 'Lord, come and see.' [35]And Jesus wept.
[36]The Jews said, 'See how he loved him!' [37]But some of them said, 'If he could open the eyes of the blind man, could he not have kept this man from dying?'
[38]Jesus was deeply moved again and drew near to the tomb. It was a cave with a stone laid across it. [39]Jesus ordered, 'Take the stone away.' Martha said to him, 'Lord, by now he will smell, for this is the fourth day.' [40]Jesus replied, 'Have I not told you that if you believe, you will see the Glory of God?' [41]So they removed the stone. Jesus lifted up his eyes and said 'Father, I thank you for you have heard me. [42]I knew that you hear me always; but my prayer was for the sake of these people, that they may believe that you sent me.' [43]When Jesus had said this, he cried out in a loud voice, 'Lazarus, come out!'
[44]The dead man came out, his hands and feet bound with linen strips and his face wrapped in a cloth. So Jesus said to them, 'Untie him and let him go.'

The raising of Lazarus was the last great public sign given by

Jesus. It was the decisive sign for the rejection or acceptance of faith in Jesus. Because he was working all these miraculous signs, the Jewish leaders made the decision that he would have to be killed. The irony was not lost on John: it was because of his power over life that Jesus was sentenced to death!

Restoring the dead to life was a miracle also associated with Elijah and Elisha in the Old Testament and with Peter and Paul in Acts. What happened in all these instances was not resurrection but resuscitation from the dead. Resuscitation means being restored or coming back to the same form of life. Resurrection is not a coming back but going forward to a new level of life beyond death.

One puzzling feature of the story is how aloof and unconcerned Jesus seems to be initially, in contrast to the intensity of his involvement once he approaches Bethany. This contrast between distance and nearness will be important for appreciating the depths of the story.

Thomas L. Brodie, in his book entitled *The Gospel according to John* (OUP, 1993), probes the significance of the two places called Bethany. There is no problem about identifying the Bethany where the family of Lazarus lived. The other Bethany, on the other side of the Jordan, was the place where John was baptising (Jn 1:28). And this was the place where Jesus was staying when news came about the illness of Lazarus (10:40). However, there is no evidence that a place called Bethany beyond the Jordan ever existed in fact.

John takes poetic licence with the name of Bethany to express the heavenly home of Jesus. In the last chapter we heard Jesus say 'I and the Father are one' (10:30). Towards the end of this chapter, Jesus thanks the Father who always hears him (11:41). The true home of Jesus is with the Father. Crossing the Jordan recalled entry in the Promised Land. In Christian terms the Promised Land is eternal life at home with Jesus, who is the resurrection and the life

In this unknown, mystical Bethany, Jesus is portrayed as distant in every sense of the word. He is emotionally distant from the great anxiety in his friend's family. His thinking is on a distant, higher plane when he says that this sickness will not end in death but in the glory of the Father.

Staying there two more days, it was on the third day, surely a link with the resurrection, that he crossed the Jordan to go to the earthly Bethany. This is the place of family and neighbours, of sickness and death, of grieving and consolation. In this real Bethany Jesus is very near and intensely involved. Three times we are told of the love he had for this family. He becomes emotionally caught up, sighing from the depths of distress and weeping.

We must consider the role of the two sisters, Martha and Mary, before we can understand the nature of his distress.

Martha went out to meet Jesus. 'If you had been here, my brother would not have died.' Words of regret, certainly. Is there an element of reproach, blaming Jesus for delaying? I do not think so, for she goes on to make a great statement of faith and trust. 'But I know that whatever you ask from God, God will give you.' Their conversation proceeds until Jesus makes his momentous statement, 'I am the resurrection; whoever believes in me, even though he die, shall live. Whoever is alive by believing in me will never die. Do you believe this?'

Martha's answer is another great act of faith. 'Yes, Lord, I have come to believe that you are the Christ, the Son of God, he who is coming into the world.' Throughout the encounter of Martha with Jesus, what dominates is her faith. Martha is the model of a faith that remains strong in the face of grief.

By contrast, the picture of Mary here shows grief dominating faith. This suggestion may come as a surprise because our familiarity with Luke 10:38-42 makes us regard Mary as the more prayerful sister.

When Mary went out to meet Jesus she was in the company of the Jews, usually a name for unbelievers in this gospel. She threw herself weeping at the feet of Jesus, the picture of unrelieved grief. We catch more than a hint of blame in their remarks, 'If he could open the eyes of the blind man, could he not have kept this man from dying?' There is no mention of faith sustaining them in their grieving.

At the sight of all this grief, Jesus was moved at a very deep level. In fact the Greek word used by the evangelist literally means snorting in breath, shuddering, almost like a horse. The usual explanation of this distress is that Jesus was totally caught up in sympathy with those who were mourning. But if our interpretation of the story as one of belief and unbelief is correct, then the deep distress of Jesus was caused by their unbelief. They were so totally clouded by grief that they no longer walked in the light of faith. Just as Jesus once wept over Jerusalem because of its lack of belief (Lk 19:41), now he was weeping because of the darkness of those whose grief caused them to forget the power of the Lord.

This interpretation of the story in terms of the light of faith and the darkness of grief helps to explain the significance of a statement of Jesus early in the chapter. 'Shall I not walk during the twelve hours of the day? Whoever walks in the daytime shall not stumble, for he sees with the light of the world. But if anyone walks by night, he will stumble for there is no light in him' (11:9-10). Martha is the model of walking with the light of faith and not stumbling, whereas the unrestrained grief of Mary causes her to stumble in the darkness of forgetting the power of the Lord.

Connecting

It is a story of many contrasts: distance and nearness; Jesus aloof and Jesus intensely involved; life and death; light and darkness; belief and unbelief.

We can identify with the experience of the distance and nearness of God. The life of faith experiences both light and darkness.

'Faith makes us taste in advance the light of the beatific vision, the goal of our journey here below. Then we shall see God "face to face", "as he is". So faith is already the beginning of eternal life' (CCC 163).

However, our experiences forcibly remind us that life here is not all light and consolation. 'Now, however, "we walk by faith, not by sight"; we perceive God as "in a mirror, dimly" and only "in part". Even though enlightened by him in whom it believes, faith is often lived in darkness and can be put to the test. The world we live in often seems very far from the one promised us by faith. Our experiences of evil and suffering, injustice, and death, seem to contradict the Good News; they can shake our faith and become a temptation against it' (CCC 164).

The dim mirror of Saint Paul's time was a metal plate which did show a reflection of sorts, quite dull and sometimes distorting the true face.

What can we do, where can we turn to when plunged into darkness at the inscrutable ways of Providence? At these times we share in the confusion of the disciples when Jesus, in the Bethany beyond the Jordan, seemed unmoved by the illness of his friend. They were further confused when he was aloof from the family anxiety and spoke about the glory of God.

The Catechism advises that in such times of confusion we should turn to the example of the great witnesses of faith in scripture and in our own experience. Abraham is a powerful witness of hope against all the odds. When God put him to the test, he was prepared to sacrifice his son, Isaac, on the strength of his belief that God would provide.

The other great scriptural model is Mary who 'in her pilgrimage of faith walked in the night of faith in sharing the darkness of her son's suffering and death' (CCC 165). Other great people down the ages have shown heroic example of courage in the face of opposition, perseverance in spite of every pressure. Viktor Frankl observed the faith of people when tested by the injustices and cruelties of the concentration camps. Suffering was like a breeze which extinguished weak faith but fanned a sturdy faith into a blazing fire.

I have witnessed great faith and inner peace in people suffering acute pain. I have been edified by the noble forgiveness shown by various victims of injustice, betrayal or cruelty. These people had a faith which sees the nearness of God inspite of the darkness. In fact, it was the very darkness which expanded their vision to see the distant stars.

Praying

Lord Jesus, you are the resurrection, the one who transcends death itself.

You are the light, whose presence sustains us from stumbling in the dark.

We pray for all whose pilgrimage has led them to the valley of darkness;

For all who experience the darkness of grief for the departure of a loved one;

For all whose faith is being tested in the night of no consolation;

For all who are suffering in body, mind or spirit,

May they know that even dark is not dark to you

And the night is as clear as the day.

John 12:1-50: Lifted Up

The Last Week

In John Chapter 12 we read of the anointing of Jesus at Bethany, his messianic entry into Jerusalem and the coming of some Greeks asking to see him. These events mark the coming of the hour of Jesus, the time of his sacrificial death and glorification.

Anointing at Bethany

[1]Six days before the Passover, Jesus came to Bethany where he had raised Lazarus, the dead man to life. [2]Now they gave a dinner for him and while Martha waited on them, Lazarus sat on the table with Jesus.
[3]Then Mary took a pound of costly perfume made from genuine nard and anointed the feet of Jesus, wiping them with her hair. And the whole house was filled with the fragrance of the perfume.
[4]Judas, son of Simon Iscariot – the disciple who was to betray Jesus – remarked, [5]This perfume could have been sold for three hundred silver coins and turned over to the poor.' [6]Judas, indeed, had no concern for the poor; he was a thief and as he held the common purse, he used to help himself to the funds.
[7]But Jesus spoke up, 'Leave her alone. Was she not keeping it for the day of my burial? [8](The poor you always have with you, but you will not always have me.)'
[9]Many Jews heard that Jesus was there and they came, not only because of Jesus, but also to see Lazarus whom he had raised from the dead. [10]So the chief priests thought about killing Lazarus as well, [11]for many of the Jews were drifting away because of him and believing in Jesus.

Jesus returned to his friends at Bethany. Lazarus, obviously restored to full appetite, gave a dinner in his honour. Busy Martha did the serving and Mary was once more drawn to the feet of

Jesus. Once she had sat there to listen to his words, but another day she had thrown herself at those feet in sheer grief. On this occasion she anointed his feet with the most expensive of ointments. Her extravagance may have been a combination of gratitude for restoring her brother and of reparation for her display of faltering faith. It was an inspired action anticipating the death of Jesus and the fact that his body would not be in the tomb for later embalming. Whatever her motive, Judas could not tune in to it. One of his failings, his dishonesty, is mentioned.

Messianic Entry

¹²The next day many people who had come for the festival heard that Jesus was to enter Jerusalem. ¹³So they took branches of palm trees and went out to meet him. And they cried out, 'Hosanna! Blessed is he who comes in the name of the Lord! Blessed is the King of Israel!'

¹⁴Jesus found a donkey and sat upon it, as Scripture says: ¹⁵Do not fear, city of Zion, see your king is coming sitting on the colt of a donkey.

¹⁶The disciples were not aware of this at first, but, after Jesus was glorified, they remembered and realized that this had been written of him and that they themselves had taken part in this.

¹⁷The people who came with him bore witness and told how he had called Lazarus out of the tomb and raised him from the dead. ¹⁸It was because of this miraculous sign which Jesus had given that so many people welcomed him. ¹⁹In the meantime the Pharisees said to one another, 'We are getting nowhere; the whole world has gone after him.'

It was expected that the Messiah would make a dramatic entry through the Golden Gate at Jerusalem to inaugurate the new kingdom. Jesus did make a processional entry but it was very low key. He rode on no magnificently caparisoned horse, which would have indicated power and domination, but on the humble donkey, symbol of peace and service. The popular expectation had not heeded the words of the prophet Zechariah: 'Rejoice greatly, daughter of Zion! Shout for joy, daughter of Jerusalem! For see, your king is coming, just and victorious, humble and riding on a donkey, on a colt, the foal of a donkey' (Zech 9:9).

The Coming of the Greeks

[20]There were some Greeks who had come up to Jerusalem to worship during the feast. [21]They approached Philip, who was from Bethsaida in Galilee, and asked him, 'Sir, we wish to see Jesus.' [22]Philip went to Andrew and the two of them told Jesus.

[23]Then Jesus said, 'The hour has come for the Son of Man to be glorified. [24]Truly, I say to you, unless the grain of wheat falls to the earth and dies, it remains alone; but if it dies, it produces much fruit.

[25]Whoever loves his life destroys it, and whoever despises his life in this world keeps it for everlasting life.

[26]Whoever wants to serve me, let him follow me and wherever I am, there shall my servant be also. If anyone serves me, the Father will honour him.

[27]Now my soul is in distress. Shall I say: "Father, save me from this hour"? But, I have come to this hour to face all this. [28]Father, glorify your Name!' Then a voice came from heaven, 'I have glorified it and I will glorify it again.'

[29]People standing there heard something and said it was thunder; but, others said, 'An angel was speaking to him.' [30]Then Jesus declared, 'This voice did not come for my sake but for yours; [31]now sentence is being passed on this world; now the ruler of this world is to be cast down. [32]And when I am lifted up from the earth, I shall draw all to myself.' [33]With these words Jesus referred to the kind of death he was to die.

[34]The crowd answered him, 'We have been told by the Law that the Messiah stands forever. How can you say that the Son of Man shall be lifted up? What kind of Son of Man is this?'

[35]Jesus said to them, 'The light will be with you a little longer. Walk while you have the light, lest the darkness overtake you. He who walks in the dark does not know where he goes. [36]While you have the light, believe in the light and become sons of light.'

After Jesus spoke, he withdrew and kept himself hidden.

The third event was the arrival of some Greeks who were anxious to see Jesus. The Pharisees were already alarmed because it seemed to them that the whole world was running after him. The coming of these Greeks marks the fulfilment of the words of Ezechiel about the Good Shepherd who would gather together the scattered sheep from foreign nations (Ezech 34:13).

John tells us no more about these Greeks but turns to the reply of Jesus. One can catch a note of excitement in his voice.

The time of preparation is nearly finished. His hour has come. His glory is about to be revealed. From the one grain buried in the earth a rich harvest would grow. The way of Jesus was through death unto his glorification. The same way must be taken by his followers. 'Whoever loves his life destroys it, and whoever despises his life in this world keeps it for everlasting life' (12:25).

Up to this, his work had been to give signs through his words and works, pointing to his divine nature and unity with the Father. Now the time for signs was completed. That is the significance of the evangelist's statement that Jesus kept himself hidden from their sight. The light would not be among them much longer.

Jesus is aware of the pains imminent in his passion. He admits to the distress he is feeling. But in John's portrait of Jesus the human pains are absorbed in the greater reality of his return to glory. The great news for us is that the glorification of Jesus is not just an event of the past but it involves us too, if we believe in him. 'And when I am lifted up from the earth, I shall draw all to myself' (12:32). John understands the lifting up of Jesus to refer to the cross as well as to his glorification.

John's summary

[37]Even though Jesus had done so many miraculous signs among them, they didn't believe in him. [38]Indeed the words of the prophet Isaiah had to be fulfilled, for he said: Lord, who has believed what we proclaimed? To whom have the ways of God the Saviour been made known?

[39]Why could they not believe? Isaiah also said: [40]He let their eyes become blind and their hearts hard, so that they could neither see nor understand. They refuse to turn to me, lest I heal them. [41]Isaiah said this when he saw His Glory, and his words refer to Him.

[42]Many of them, however, believed in Jesus, even among the rulers, but they did not acknowledge him because of the Pharisees, lest they be put out of the Jewish community. [43]They preferred to be approved by people rather than by God.

[44]Yet Jesus had said, and even cried out, 'He who believes in me, believes not in me but in him who sent me. [45]And he who sees me,

sees him who sent me. ⁴⁶I have come into the world as light, so that whoever believes in me may not remain in darkness.

⁴⁷If anyone hears my words and does not keep them, I am not the one to condemn him; for, I have come not to condemn the world but to save the world. ⁴⁸He who rejects me, and does not receive my word, already has a judge: the very word I have spoken will condemn him on the last day.

⁴⁹For I have not spoken on my own authority; the Father who sent me has instructed me in what to say and how to speak. ⁵⁰I know that his commandment is eternal life, and I give my message as the Father instructed me.'

The evangelist then reflects on the signs given by Jesus. Many closed their eyes and hearts to his light. And there were some among the Jews who did believe but lacked the courage to profess it openly, preferring human popularity to the honour of God. The words and works of Jesus were signs pointing beyond to the Father who had sent him. 'He who believes in me, believes not in me but in him who sent me. And he who sees me, sees him who sent me' (45-46). People will be their own judges according to their acceptance or rejection of the light of Jesus.

Connecting

'When I am lifted up from the earth, I shall draw all people to myself' (12:32). Jesus was referring to the cross on which he would be lifted up before the eyes of the world.

He draws but does not coerce our human response. Down the ages people have been drawn into the love of Christ through prayer before the cross. Francis of Assisi spoke of the cross as a book.

We see Jesus lifted up before our eyes. Totally given to the Father's will. And totally given up for love of us. Greater love no one can show than to lay down one's life for others.

He opened his arms on the cross in a worldwide invitation and embrace. Having loved those who were his in the world, he loved them to the end. He is utterly defenceless, clutching no weapons in retaliation, clenching no fist in anger. He prays for his persecutors. Love has triumphed over hatred and bitterness.

In the weakness of death he shows the divine power of resurrection. In the foolishness of love he proves the wisdom of God.

In the light of the cross we see our own lives. For if the cross of Christ carries the greatest manifestation of love, then the greatest contradiction of the cross is selfishness. The cross shows up how proud and arrogant we are. Bossy and tyrannical. Mean and selfish. Insensitive and hurtful. Judgemental and unforgiving.

Lifted up from the earth, his love draws us from our sins and lifts us up to sharing in his life and reproducing his virtues.

Praying

Lord Jesus, lifted up on the cross before our eyes, we ponder your total love. In your wounds we see the ugly consequences of sin. In your outstretched arms we see the embrace of your love. Draw us through your open side that we might ever reside in your heart of love.

Risen Lord Jesus, lifted up in your return to the Father, we praise you. Lift us up, draw us out of our fallen, wounded condition. Raise us up in hope when darkness and fear surround us. Strengthen us to live with virtues that reflect the beauty of your love in the world.

Bestow your Holy Spirit upon us with the power to be true children of the Father, raised up to the fullness of human potential in divine adoption.

John 13: Before the Passover

Chapter Thirteen is about two journeys: the return of Jesus to the Father in the fulfilment of the Passover; and the sad journey of Judas towards the outer darkness.

The Passover of Jesus

[1]It was before the feast of the Passover. Jesus realized that his hour had come to pass from this world to the Father, and, as he had loved those who were his own in the world, he would love them with perfect love.

[2]They were at supper; the devil had already put into the mind of Judas son of Simon Iscariot, to betray him [3]but Jesus knew that the Father had entrusted all things to him and, as he had come from God, he was going to God. [4]So he got up from table, removed his garment and taking a towel wrapped it around his waist. [5]Then he poured water into a basin and began to wash the disciples' feet and to wipe them with the towel he was wearing.

[6]When he came to Simon Peter, Simon said to him, 'Why, Lord, you want to wash my feet!' [7]Jesus said, 'What I am doing you cannot understand now, but afterwards you will understand it.' [8]Peter replied, You shall never wash my feet.' Jesus answered him, 'If I do not wash you, you can have no part with me.' [9]Then Simon Peter said, 'Lord, wash not only my feet, but also my hands and my head!' [10]Jesus replied,'Whoever has taken a bath does not need to wash (except the feet), for he is clean all over. You are clean, though not all of you.' [11]Jesus knew who was to betray him; because of this he said, 'Not all of you are clean.'

[12]When Jesus had finished washing their feet, he put on his garment again, went back to the table and said to them, 'Do you understand what I have done to you?' [13]You call me Master and Lord, and you are right, for so I am. [14]If I, then, your Lord and Master, have washed your feet, you also must wash one another's feet. [15]I have just given you an example that as I have done, you also may do.

JOHN 13: BEFORE THE PASSOVER

> [16]Truly, I say to you, the servant is not greater than his master, nor is the messenger greater than he who sent him. [17]Understand this, and blessed are you if you put it into practice.
> [18]I am not speaking of you all, because I know the ones I have chosen and the Scripture has to be fulfilled that says, The one who shared my table has risen against me. [19]I tell you this now before it happens, you may know that I am He.
> [20]Truly, I say to you, whoever welcomes the one I send, welcomes me, and whoever welcomes me, welcomes the One who sent me.'

'It was before the feast of Passover.' We have already seen the significance of Jewish feasts in understanding the actions of Jesus. Two other events, the clearing of the Temple (2:13) and the miracle of the loaves (6:4) took place in the same time-setting, just before the Passover of the Jews. However, on this third occurrence of the feast, John omits the phrase 'of the Jews' because the story he is about to relate is the passing of Jesus from this world to the Father. It is important for John that it took place before the feast because in his chronology the death of Jesus took place on the day before the feast (19:31), when the paschal lambs were being sacrificed.

The Passover commemorated the journey of the Hebrew people from slavery in Egypt to freedom in the promised land. That great journey is about to be replaced by the journey of Jesus, who had come from the Father, back to the Father (13:3).

Love was the motive that inspired his coming and going. 'God so loved the world that he gave his only Son ...' (3:16). And his return from the world to the Father was to be through a sacrificial death which would show how perfect or total his love was. As the Good Shepherd who cared for his flock, he would freely lay down his life and take it up again (10:18). These actions are recalled in his gestures as he lay down his outer garment and took up a towel. The towel was wrapped round his waist like the binding of a slave.

Washing the feet of the disciples was both a symbolic act of purification and an example of humble service. As a rite of cleansing before a meal it was a symbol of our need to be purified of sin by Jesus before a life of union with him. 'If I do not wash you, you can have no part with me' (13:8). This may be an allusion to the water of baptism. As Jesus indicated in his response to Peter, in a symbolic washing a token amount of water is sufficient to express the meaning of the act.

The lesson of humble service is an extraordinary action. Though Lord and Master, he had come to serve and to lay down his life in love for the flock. His example is a model of how his followers ought to behave.

Judas

[21] After saying this, Jesus was distressed in spirit and said plainly, 'Truly, one of you will betray me.' [22] The disciples then looked at one another, wondering who he meant. [23] One of the disciples, the one Jesus loved, was reclining near Jesus; [24] so Simon Peter signaled him to ask Jesus whom he meant.

[25] And the disciple who was reclining near Jesus asked him, 'Lord, who is it?' [26] Jesus answered, 'I shall dip a piece of bread in the dish, and he to whom I give it, is the one.'

So Jesus dipped the bread and gave it to Judas Iscariot the son of Simon. [27] And as Judas took the piece of bread, Satan entered into him. And Jesus said to him, 'What you are going to do, do quickly.' [28] None of the others reclining at table understood why Jesus said this to Judas. [29] As he had the common purse, they may have thought that Jesus was telling him, 'Buy what we need for the feast', or 'Give something to the poor.' [30] Judas left as soon as he had eaten the bread. It was night.

The loving service of Jesus is in stark contrast with the option of Judas for the way that led to outer darkness. The devil had already put it into his mind to betray Jesus (13:2). The devil cannot enter the will directly but planted the notion in his mind. Judas was still free to reject the temptation. But once he made his decision he opened the door of his will and Satan entered him (13:27). When Judas went out from that table-fellowship night had fallen (13:30). A dreadful description of a soul that had rejected the light of the Lord.

Reflection

³¹When Judas had gone out, Jesus said, 'Now is the Son of Man glorified and God is glorified in him. ³²So God will glorify him, and he will glorify him very soon.
³³My children, I am with you for only a little while; you will look for me, but, as I already told the Jews, so now I tell you: where I am going you cannot come. ³⁴Now I give you a new commandment: love one another. Just as I have loved you, you also must love one another. ³⁵By this everyone will know that you are my disciples, if you have love for one another.'
³⁶Simon Peter said to him, 'Lord, where are you going?' Jesus answered, 'Where I am going you cannot follow me now, but afterwards you will.' ³⁷Peter said, 'Why can't I follow you now? I am ready to give my life for you.' ³⁸Jesus answer, 'To give your life for me! Truly, I tell you, the cock will not crow before you have denied me three times.'

The departure of Judas about his nefarious business set in motion the train of events that would lead Jesus to the cross. But the broader view sees Jesus going to the glory of the Father.

He would not be with the disciples physically for much longer. But they would always find him present in their lives if they followed the example of his love and service. He called it a new commandment. It was new, not as if the Old Testament had not spoken of love and kindness already, but in the standard of love set in the example of Jesus and in the power to love with a sharing in God's own love.

Connecting

There is an essential link between the washing of the disciples' feet, which John emphasises at the last supper, and the institution of the Eucharist, which the other evangelists highlight.

Mark, Matthew and Luke give us the moral teaching of Jesus during his public mission and the institution of the Eucharist at the last supper, whereas John gives the teaching on the Eucharist during the public ministry and the moral teaching at the supper. There is, in fact, very little moral teaching in John beyond the general instruction to obey the commandments and this lesson of loving service. The principle behind the sacraments, the use of everyday matter like bread, water or wine as the medium of divine power, runs right through his writing.

The time-setting, before the feast of Passover, is a connecting link between the washing of the feet and the eucharistic teaching of Chapter 6. Furthermore, the first mention of the betrayal of Judas is at the time when many of the disciples rejected the eucharistic teaching (6:71) while his final decision to betray Jesus is at the supper.

The liturgy of Holy Thursday preserves the connection between the institution of the Eucharist and the washing of the feet of the disciples. The Eucharist is at the same time a meal which expresses the unity of those at table as well as being the food which strengthens people to go from the table to greater works of love, humble service and unification.

The word *communion* derives from the word *munus*, meaning a burden or responsibility. *Com-munio* literally means a shared task or mission. At the end of Mass, those who have heard the word of the Lord and who have been nourished in the Eucharist are sent out on a mission to love and serve the Lord. As Mass ends, mission begins. The message and love of Jesus Christ which were celebrated at the tables of word and banquet must not be locked up in the church. The Eucharist is not complete until Christ's love is brought out to others in practical service. That was something deeply understood by Mother Teresa of Calcutta.

'No one has ever seen God,
but if we love one another, God lives in us,
and his love spreads freely among us' (1 Jn 4:12).
God's love for us is completed only when we pass it on to others.

Praying

Jesus, Lord and Master!
You are Lord in your divinity. In love you came down to us from on high to lift us up with you in your return to the Father's glory.

You are Master in your teaching, especially in your example of selfless love ... washing the feet of the disciples and laying down your life for the flock.

Wash us as once you washed your disciples. Cleanse us of any defilement that would prevent us from belonging to you. Cleanse us of the traces of sin which weaken us.

In the sacred bread which you give us, strengthen us against the wiles of Satan. May we never reject you by choosing the ways that lead to darkness.

Jesus, Lord and Master, we adore you and we love you.

John 14: Motives for consolation

The last supper discourse in John extends over three chapters which deal with:
- the consolation of the disciples at the imminent departure of Jesus (Chapter 14);
- the vine and the branches (Chapter 15);
- encouragement for the future (Chapter 16).

Preparing a place

¹Do not be troubled; you believe in God, believe also in me. ²In my Father's house there are many rooms and I go to prepare a place for you: did I not tell you this? ³And as I go now to prepare a place for you, I shall come again and take you to me, that where I am, you also may be.
⁴You know the way to where I am going.' ⁵Thomas said to him, 'Lord, we don't know where you are going; how can we know the way?' ⁶Jesus said, 'I am the way, (the truth and the life;) no one comes to the Father but through me. ⁷If you know me, you will know the Father also; indeed you know him and you have seen him.'
⁸Philip asked him, 'Lord, show us the Father and that is enough.' ⁹Jesus said to him,'What! I have been with you so long and you still do not know me, Philip? Whoever sees me sees the Father; how can you say: 'Show us the Father'? ¹⁰Do you not believe that I am in the Father and the Father in me?
All that I say to you, I do not say of myself. The Father who dwells in me is doing his work. ¹¹Believe me when I say that I am in the Father and the Father in me; at least believe it on the evidence of these works that I do.

Chapter Fourteen contains five great teachings of Jesus for the consolation of the disciples in their sadness and confusion at the prospect of his departure.

Jesus appeals to them to continue to trust him. His departure must not shake their faith as he is, in fact, going to the Father to prepare a place for them. And this is the first motive of consolation. There will be no shortage of space there, plenty of room. He will come again to take to himself those who live according to his way.

The questions asked by Thomas about the way allows Jesus to assert, 'I am the way, the truth and the life.' He is the way whose teaching guides our behaviour and shows us how to live. He is the truth in whom the searching mind will find ultimate meaning and satisfaction. He is the life who has conquered death and offers eternal life to all who accept his way and truth. There is no other way to the Father but through Jesus.

When Philip sighs audibly in his desire to see the Father. Jesus replies that to have seen him is to have seen the Father. Human eyes would be incapable of enduring the direct vision of God. Jesus is the human revelation of God, the word made flesh. This is one of the key themes of John and the reason why he is compared to the eagle, which is reputed to be the only creature capable of looking directly into the light of the sun. In knowing Jesus and his works one is able to see what God is like.

Greater days ahead

[12]Truly, I say to you, he who believes in me will do the same works that I do; he will even do greater than these, for I am going where the Father is. [13]And everything you ask in my name, I will do, so that the Father may be glorified in the Son. [14]And everything you ask in calling upon my Name, I will do.

The second motive for hope is that greater works will be seen in the days after the return of Jesus to the Father, that is, in the time of the church. How could these latter times possibly be greater than the days of Jesus in the flesh? In the vertical sense of prayer in the name of Jesus and in the horizontal sense of the greater geographical outreach of the Christian mission.

The prayer of disciples would have a new power. 'And everything you ask in my name, I will do, so that the Father may be glorified in the Son.' Jesus, lifted up from the earth in glory, raises up the believer into participating in his own glorification of the Father. The risen Lord is ever living to intercede for all who come to the Father through him (Heb 7:25). Prayer in the name of Jesus means to be united with him in his return to the Father. This is most perfectly realised in the liturgy of the Eucharist in which the believer is caught up in the Word's timeless expression of the glory of the Father. Through him, with him and in him, all glory and honour are rendered to the Father in the power of the Holy Spirit. Prayer in the name of Jesus means participating with him in person. Indeed, all liturgical prayer is offered in the name of Jesus.

In the horizontal sense of reaching out to others, the time of the church is a mission to all nations and ages, whereas the mission of Jesus' own day was confined to a small region and to a few short years. The mission of Jesus has now acquired countless feet, hands, mouths and hearts to give greater extent to his deeds.

The Holy Spirit

[15]If you love me, you will keep my commandments; [16]and I will ask the Father and he will give you another Helper to be with you forever, [17]that Spirit of truth whom the world cannot receive because it neither sees him nor knows him. But you know him for he is with you and will be in you.

The third consolation is in the promise of the Holy Spirit as the *Paraclete* (Greek) or *Advocatus* (Latin), meaning someone called beside you. The Holy Spirit is God's love ever beside one, the divine friend who whispers comfort to the heart and light to the mind. To be comforted literally means to be strong with *(cum-fortis)* the support of somebody. A comforter is one who brings inner strength. The promise of Jesus is that the Holy Spirit, as the Spirit of truth, would give immense inner strength to all who believe. The eternal truth of the word of God is the source of unflinching strength in the face of all contradiction.

Divine adoption and indwelling

¹⁸I will not leave you orphans, I am coming to you. ¹⁹A little while and the world will see me no more, but you will see me because I live and you will also live. ²⁰On that day you will know that I am in my Father and you in me, and I in you.
²¹Whoever keeps my commandments is the one who loves me. If he loves me, he will also be loved by my Father; I too shall love him and show myself clearly to him.'
²²Judas – not the Iscariot – asked Jesus, 'Lord, how can it be that you will show yourself clearly to us and not to the world?' ²³Jesus answered him, 'If anyone loves me, he will keep my word and my Father will love him and we will come to him and make our home with him. ²⁴But if anyone does not love me, he will not keep my words. And these words that you hear are not mine but the Father's who sent me.
²⁵I told you all this while I was still with you. ²⁶From now on the Helper, the Holy Spirit whom the Father will send in my name, will teach you all things and remind you of all that I have told you.

The fourth motive is the promise of Jesus not to leave his followers orphaned. In a little while they would no longer have his physical presence. To the unbeliever this would be similar to being orphaned. But people who believe in Jesus and keep his commandments would be raised by adoption into divine life, being given the power to become the children of God (1:12).

In a short while Jesus would no longer be there for the world or physical eye to see, but he would come back to the disciples after his resurrection and they would see him in the sense of believing in his presence.

The question put by Judas, not Iscariot, invites Jesus to make a further clarification. Whoever loves Jesus and sets up home in his words (8:31) will find that God is as near as one's own heart. This is the doctrine of the divine indwelling. No longer would Jesus be seen and heard with the outer senses but the Spirit dwelling within would enable the disciples to understand more fully all that Jesus had taught.

True peace

²⁷Peace be with you; I give you my peace. Not as the world gives peace do I give it to you. Do not be troubled; do not be afraid. ²⁸You heard me say: "I am going away, but I am coming to you". If you loved me, you would be glad that I go to the Father, for the Father is greater than I.
²⁹I have told you this now before it takes place, so that when it does happen you may believe, ³⁰for I will no longer speak to you. Now the ruler of this world is at hand, although there is nothing in me that he can claim.
³¹But see, the world must know that I love the Father and that I do what the Father has taught me to do. Come now, let us go.

The fifth motive for consolation is the gift of Christ's peace. On the very eve of his suffering, Jesus spoke of peace. The peace which the world gives comes from outer circumstances such as the absence of war, violence, injustice, hardship or pain. The peace of Jesus is an inner strength shown in serenity even in the face of impending violence and suffering. The Spirit dwelling within is the source of that peace.

The chapter closes with a brief reminder that the departure of Jesus is really a glad occasion because he is going to the Father. Satan, the prince of this world, is about to have his fling through unleashing the injustice and violence of enemies on Jesus. But Jesus is totally free and enters the passion in loving obedience to the plan of the Father.

Connecting

This is a chapter of great consolation, hope, strength and peace. If I am conscious in my last hours of life, my great desire is that somebody will read these words for me. Do not be troubled; trust in God and trust in me. I go now to prepare a place for you ... I shall come again to take you to me.

Hope is not only for life after death but is also the strength for here and now. The words of Jesus ask the disciples to move forward from the time of his physical presence as the way of seeing God to the time when the Holy Spirit would be the source of faith. The presence of Jesus in human flesh on earth was for a short few years, but his glorification would release the Holy Spirit for all ages, to be within all who love Jesus and observe his teaching.

Up to recent years the role of the Holy Spirit in our lives was seriously neglected. The Spirit was the forgotten Paraclete. It is one of the great seeds of hope for the church today that people have become far more aware of the presence and power of the Spirit.

I have heard people describe their experience of the indwelling Spirit as an eighteen inch drop, the distance from the head into the heart: from a remote God out there to an experience of God within; from a brain-centred prayer battling with distractions, to an awareness of God in the happenings of everyday life.

God is at the centre of our being. Constant prayer develops the habit of attentiveness to God. Perhaps there is too much babbling in words, too much chasing off to different places. All the while God is within the sanctified soul. What we need in the bustling, noisy world of today is inner silence to nurture attentiveness to God within.

Many people have found great help in some simple focus such as with an icon or a mantra to supply a homing point for the distracted mind. 'Make your home in my word' (8:31). Uncomplicated awareness of God is the characteristic mark of contemplative prayer.

'Entering into contemplative prayer is like entering into the Eucharistic liturgy: we 'gather up' the heart, recollect our whole being under the prompting of the Holy Spirit, abide in the dwelling place of the Lord which we are, awaken our faith in order to enter into the presence of him who awaits us. We let our masks fall and turn our hearts back to the Lord who loves us, so as to hand ourselves over to him as an offering to be purified and transformed' (CCC 2711).

Praying

Lord Jesus, we thank you for the great consolations of our faith. You have transformed death, you have opened up the mansions of heaven, you have gone to prepare a place for us.

In your eternal return to the Father you now do not go alone. Having become our brother in human flesh you have raised up to divine life all who love you and observe your words. Your glorification has released the Holy Spirit like a wellspring in the heart.

O Blessed Paraclete, you are the Friend beside us and within us. You comfort, strengthen and enlighten. May we grow in awareness of your presence. May we discern where you lead us. May we be active instruments of divine love.

John 15: The True Vine

The early pruning

[1]I am the true vine and my Father is the vinegrower. [2]If any of my branches doesn't bear fruit, he breaks it off; and he prunes every branch that does bear fruit, that it may bear even more fruit.

[3]You are already made clean by the word I have spoken to you; [4]live in me as I live in you. The branch cannot bear fruit by itself but has to remain part of the vine; so neither can you if you don't remain in me.

[5]I am the vine and you are the branches. As long as you remain in me and I in you, you bear much fruit; but apart from me you can do nothing. [6]Whoever does not remain in me is like a branch that is thrown away and withers; and the withered branches are thrown into the fire and burned.

[7]If you remain in me and my words in you, you may ask whatever you want and it will be given to you. [8]My Father is glorified when you become my disciples, that is, when you bear much fruit.

[9]As the Father has loved me, so I have loved you; remain in my love. [10]You will remain in my love if you keep my commandments, just as I have kept my Father's commandments and remain in his love.

[11]I have told you all this, that my own joy may be in you and your joy may be complete. [12]This is my commandment; love one another as I have loved you. [13]There is no greater love than this, to give one's life for his friends; [14]and you are my friends if you do what I command you.

[15]I shall not call you servants any more, because a servant does not know what his master is about. Instead I call you friends since I have made known to you everything I learned from my Father.

[16]You did not choose me; it was I who chose you and sent you to go and bear much fruit, fruit that will last. For everything you ask the Father in my name, he will give you.

[17]So I tell you to love one another.

The image of the vine or vineyard had been used frequently in the Old Testament for the chosen people. In one particular passage, Jeremiah lamented how this chosen vine had become a wild, degenerate plant. Jesus has already identified himself as the Good Shepherd, in contrast to the bad pastors, and now he is claiming to be the True Vine, as opposed to the degenerate one. Once again, John has Jesus giving new meaning to some revered symbol of the Jews.

The disciples are identified as the branches called to bear fruit and the Father is the vinedresser. The vine is a plant that needs a severe pruning in early spring, otherwise it will send out too many wild and fruitless branches. With regard to the disciples of Jesus, this spring pruning had already taken place in their acceptance of his word. 'You are already made clean by the word I have spoken to you.' His teaching on the Bread of Life in Chapter Six was the cut-off point for many who no longer walked with him.

Having been chosen to survive the first pruning, the disciples are told that they must remain firmly united to Jesus. Apart from him they would be powerless. The message of remaining in him is so important that Jesus repeats it ten times.

Remaining in Jesus will be manifested in keeping his commandments, especially the new commandment of love according to the standard of his self-sacrificing love.

Whoever remains united to the words and love of Jesus will grow in intimate relationship with him, advancing from service to the sort of friendship where minds meet in union.

The branches are destined to bear fruit as the disciples are commissioned, that is called to share in the mission of Jesus. Again Jesus speaks of the power of prayer in his name.

The later pruning

[18]If the world hates you, remember that the world hated me before you. [19]This would not be so if you belonged to the world, because the world loves its own. But you are not of the world since I have chosen you from the world; because of this the world hates you.
[20]Remember what I told you: the servant is not greater that his master; if they persecute me, they will persecute you, too. Have they kept my teaching? Will they then keep yours? [21]All this they will do

to you for the sake of my name because they do not know the One who sent me.
²²If I had not come to tell them, they would have no sin, but now they have no excuse for their sin. ²³Those who hate me hate my Father.
²⁴If I had not done among them what no one else has ever done, they would have no sin. But after they have seen, they hate me and my Father, ²⁵and the words written in their law become true: They hated me without cause.
²⁶I will send you from the Father, the Spirit of truth who comes from the Father. When this Helper comes, he will testify about me. ²⁷And you, too, will be my witnesses for you have been with me from the beginning.

A second pruning of the vine is done in August, a month before harvesting. The branches which carry little or no fruit are pinched out so as to let more sap swell out the stronger fruit. This later pruning refers to the time after Jesus when the disciples would meet with hatred and persecution from the unbelieving world. Soon they would see what blind hatred would do to Jesus. That same hatred would later unleash persecution against those who followed the word of Jesus.

Jesus returns to his teaching in the previous chapter that in the days after his life on earth the strength of his followers would come from the Holy Spirit.

Connecting

This is a chapter of extraordinary I-You intimacy between Jesus and his followers. There are more than twenty statements of this relationship. The poetic imagery of the vineyard echoes the lover's rhapsody in the Song of Songs. Jesus the Lover invites the beloved to live at home in his life and love. His words are to be heard by every follower as a personal message of love.

Remain ... abide ... set up home ... however we translate the idea, it is heard ten times to bring out the many nuances of lovers' union.

I have loved you as the Father loves me.

I have loved you to the point of laying down my life for you.

I wish to share the fullness of my joy with you.
I call you friends.
I have made known to you everything I learnt from my Father.
I chose you.
I send you out to bear fruit.

One should spend time with each of these love messages in turn. Hear the Lord say them to you personally. You are called not just to serve the Lord but to enjoy his love and friendship.

Philosophers tell us that it is principally in the experience of I-Thou relationships that we come to know our identity. My identity as a Christian grows with the deepening appreciation that I am loved ... I am called to his joy ... I am his friend ... I am guided by his commandments ... I am chosen ... I share his mission to bear fruit.

If we are overwhelmed by our unworthiness it is consoling to notice that the part of the vine or any fruit tree which bears the fruit is the most fragile, breakable tip of the branch. In the wonderful ways of the providence, God has chosen humble people, who know their own weakness and their dependence on God, to bear fruit.

Many of the heroes of the bible had sinful backgrounds. Moses had killed a man and buried him in the sand, yet he was chosen by God to lead the people out of bondage in Egypt. David was guilty of adultery, of deception and of causing many deaths in an unnecessary battle to cover up his tracks. Yet he is remembered as the ideal king and his name is associated with the psalms. Peter denied all contact with Jesus, yet he was the chosen rock on which Christ built his church. Paul as a religious fanatic hunted down the followers of Jesus before he became the apostle of the Mediterranean lands and the first great theologian in the church.

In the life of Francis of Assisi, his handsome companion, Brother Masseo, half jokingly asked why the people were flocking to Francis who lacked good looks and attractive voice. Francis replied that in all the world God could not find anybody more vile and contemptible, so that it might be clear to all that what was happening was entirely due to God and not to any attributes of his. That is humility, down to earth truthfulness.

Humble people know their dependence. Francis once marvelled at the reflection of a tree in a puddle. In the reflection he saw the tree upside down, as it were hanging from the sky. He understood how total is our dependence on God. True followers of Jesus know that their roots are in him and that they can do nothing apart from him. They constantly strive to remain tuned in to the word of God. And they experience the presence of the Spirit within them, empowering them to witness to God's love and thus bear fruit in the world.

Praying

Lord Jesus, you are the vine and we are the branches. Apart from you we can do nothing. Grant us the grace to persevere ... to remain in you ... to remain true to your word ... to remain in your love ... to experience the fullness of your joy.

To be your servant, Lord, is a great honour; but to hear you call us Friend is beyond anything we might merit. It is a calling born out of the love in your heart.

In your friendship you have chosen us and blessed us with your divine word. You have given us the privilege of working in your name and commissioned us to bear fruit.

We pray for all who face hostility, hatred or opposition because of their loyalty to you. May they know that they are following in your footsteps as you too were rejected by many.

Send your promised Spirit into our hearts to be our inner light and strength.

John 16: Time after Jesus

¹I tell you all this to keep you from stumbling and falling away ²when you are put out of the Jewish communities. The hour is coming when anyone who kills you will claim to be serving God; ³they will do this because they have not known the Father or me. ⁴Now I tell you all these things so that when the time comes you may remember that I told you.

I did not tell you this in the beginning because I was with you. ⁵But now I am going to the One who sent me and none of you asks me where I am going, ⁶for you are overcome with grief because of what I said.

⁷Indeed believe me: It is better for you that I go away, because as long as I do not leave, the Helper will not come to you; but I am going away and then I will send him to you.

⁸When he comes, he will uncover the lie of the world and show clearly what its sin has been, what the way of righteousness is, and how the Judgement has come.

⁹What has its sin been? They did not believe in me. ¹⁰What is the way of righteousness? The One you see no more has gone directly to the Father. ¹¹How has the Judgement come? The Ruler of this world has himself been condemned.

¹²I still have many things to tell you, but you cannot bear them now. ¹³When he, the Spirit of truth comes, he will guide you into the whole truth.

He will not give his own message but will speak only of what he hears, and he will tell you of the things to come. ¹⁴He will take what is mine and make it known to you; in doing this he will glorify me. ¹⁵All that the Father has is mine; because of this I have just told you, that the Spirit will take what is mine and make it known to you.'

¹⁶'A little while and you will see me no more; and than a little while and you will see me.'

Many of the consoling thoughts of Chapter 14 are repeated in Chapter 16 but in a different context. The former chapter was in the context of the imminent departure of Jesus with all its attendant sadness and confusion; the focus of the latter chapter is on the plight of the disciples in the difficult days after the going away of Jesus. The evangelist was writing for a people who had suffered at the hands of the mainstream Jewish leaders who rejected the claims of Jesus. Synagogues were closed to them and they experienced persecution, supposedly in God's name.

While the disciples were sad because Jesus was talking about going away, he told them that they must be willing to let go and to move on. They must let go of the time of his physical presence and move on to the days of the Spirit. Earlier, in John 7:38, the evangelist commented that the Spirit was not yet given because Jesus was not yet glorified.

One of the functions of the Holy Spirit would be as Advocate in the legal sense, establishing the justice of Jesus and how wrong his accusers were about sin, about righteousness and about judgement.

In John's gospel the essence of sin is in not believing in Jesus. The Holy Spirit would show how wrong was their refusal to believe. That Jesus was totally in the right would be proved by his going to the Father. And the Spirit would show up how the judgement against Jesus was the work of Satan, once the prince of this world, but whose reign was overthrown in the death and rising of Jesus. In the days after Jesus, the Holy Spirit would unmask all the lies and let the complete truth be seen.

John 16:17-33
> [17]Some of the disciples wondered, 'What does he mean by: "A little while and you will not see me, and then a little while and you will see me"? And why did he say: "I go to the Father"?' [18]And they said to one another, 'What does he mean by "a little while"?' We don't understand.'
> [19]Jesus realized that they wanted to question him; so he said to them, 'You are puzzled because I told you that in a little while you will see me no more, and then a little while later you will see me.
> [20]Truly, I say to you, you will weep and mourn while the world rejoices. You will be sorrowful, but your sorrow will turn to joy.
> [21]A woman in childbirth is in distress because her time is at hand.

But after the child is born, she no longer remembers her suffering because of such joy: a man is born into the world.
²²So you feel sorrowful now, but I will see you again; and your hearts will rejoice in such a way that no one will take your joy from you. ²³In that day you will not ask me anything. Truly, I say to you, whatever you ask the Father in my Name, he will give you. ²⁴So far you have not asked in my Name; so ask and receive that your joy may be full.
²⁵I taught you all this in veiled language, but the time is coming when I shall no longer speak in veiled language, but will tell you plainly of the Father.
²⁶In that day you will ask in my Name and it will not be for me to ask the Father for you, ²⁷for the Father himself loves you because you have loved me and you believe that I came from the Father. ²⁸As I came from the Father and have come into the world, so I am leaving the world and going to the Father.'
²⁹The disciples said to him, 'Now you are speaking plainly and not in veiled language! ³⁰Now we see that you know all things, even before we question you. Because of this we believe that you came from God.'
³¹Jesus answered them, 'You say that you believe! ³²The hour is coming, indeed it has come, when you will be scattered each one to his home, and you will leave me alone. Yet I am not alone, for the Father is with me.
³³I have told you all this, so that in me you may have peace, even though you have trouble in the world. Courage! I have overcome the world.'

Another motive for consolation is offered in comparing the suffering of Jesus and of his disciples to the labour pains of a woman at childbirth. Her suffering is soon forgotten in the joy of new life. The disciples would find their sadness transformed into total joy once they understood where he was going. And since he was going to the Father, their prayer, offered in his name, was guaranteed a new efficacy.

A perfect summary of the twofold journey of Jesus, down and up, is given in John 16:28. 'As I came from the Father and have come into the world, so I am leaving the world and going to the Father.' There is a paradox at the centre of Christianity.

Jesus had to come down to us in order to lift us up. Out of his death comes eternal life. From the wheat grain dying in the ground sprouts a rich harvest. Out of voluntary poverty sprouts enrichment. Out of excessive self-love comes the loss of life's potential whereas it is by letting go of life that one keeps it for the eternal life.

The final message is one of encouragement. Jesus predicts the troubles they would have to face but he exhorts them to be full of faith and courage 'for I have overcome the world'. The victory of Jesus is the guarantee of future joy for his beleaguered followers.

Connecting

'As I came from the Father and have come into the world, so I am leaving the world and going to the Father' (16:28). One day of illumination, more than thirty years ago, this verse was part of a process which opened up for me a whole new understanding of the mystery of the Eucharist in terms of the journey of Jesus Christ returning to the Father.

Up to that, I had understood the sacrifice of Christ only in terms of his death. Our theology at that time said nothing about his going to the Father in his resurrection-ascension as part of his sacrifice. Yet the essence of sacrifice is not in the self-denial, even in death, but in the giving to God. *Sacrum-facere* means to give something to God. Death alone was incomplete without the resurrection and return to the Father.

Our theology of the Eucharist concentrated so much on the question of transubstantiation that the link with the biblical idea of the Exodus and Passover was overlooked. The evangelist John emphasised how Jesus brought the Passover celebration of the Exodus to its fulfilment in his passing from this world to the Father.

John tells the whole story of Jesus as a journey in three stages. Jesus came down to us, lived among us and then returned to the Father. These dynamic movements of John's gospel are like the three lines of a triangle. The first line, descending from the apex, represents the coming down of Jesus into our world. 'Yes, God so loved the word that he gave his only Son...' (3:16). The base line represents our level of life. 'And the Word was made flesh; he had his tent pitched among us ...' (1:14). He entered human life, accepting limitations and suffering. At the end of this line place the cross where his earthly life expired. But the cross was not the end of the story and the triangle is not complete until a line ascends to connect again with the apex. The journey of Jesus was not completed until his return to the Father. 'As I came from the Father and have come into the world, so I am leaving the world and going to the Father' (16:28).

This completion of the journey of Jesus is the fulfilment of what had been foreshadowed in the Jewish Passover which celebrated the work of God in leading the people out of the slavery of Egypt, through the Red Sea, into freedom and a land of their own. The time-setting for the last supper discourse was 'before the festival of the Passover when Jesus knew that the hour had come for him to pass from this world to the Father' (13:1). Just as he had previously given new meaning to Sabbath, Tabernacles and Dedication, now he is bringing out the meaning that was foreshadowed by the earlier Passover.

The Passover of Jesus is known to us as the Paschal Mystery and it is at the heart of Christian liturgy. In dying Jesus destroyed death. His actions are part of an eternal present. All that Jesus did 'participates in the divine eternity and so transcends all times while being made present in them all' (CCC 1084).

Christian liturgy is a celebration of the timeless acts of Jesus Christ in raising up humanity to the supernatural life of becoming children of God. At the heart of the eucharistic liturgy we remember the death, resurrection and ascension of the Lord Jesus. To remember in the biblical sense is to believe that the power of God shown in the past event is present in this celebration. 'Christ Jesus is the same today as yesterday and forever' (Heb 13:8).

'Christian liturgy not only recalls the events that saved us but actualises them, makes them present. The Paschal Mystery of Christ is celebrated, not repeated. It is the celebrations that are repeated, and in each celebration there is an outpouring of the Holy Spirit that makes the unique mystery present' (CCC 1104).

To pray in the name of Jesus acquires its full significance only when worshippers are united with Jesus in his return to the Father. In the inner movements of the Blessed Trinity, Jesus, the Word, is the image of the Father's glory, the perfect copy of his nature. Only through Jesus is there access to the Father's glory and it is in this that Christian liturgy participates. Lifted up from the earth he draws all people to himself.

Praying

Risen Lord Jesus, like the first disciples we too experience times of sadness, loneliness and confusion when we long for the touch of your nearness. May we never doubt the presence of your Holy Spirit in our hearts. May we be sensitive to the Spirit's divine whisper and gentle movements.

We take into our prayer all who are suffering in any way, especially those in depression of spirit. May they experience the consolations of your Spirit who does not leave us orphaned. May they know that they are not alone on the road of suffering for you have made the cross the way to resurrection. Fill us with that courage which comes from knowing that you have overcome all evil.

Lord Jesus, we celebrate your return to glory with the Father. And we rejoice in our belief that you raise us up to participate in the eternal praises of heaven. When we eat this bread and drink this cup, we proclaim your death, Lord Jesus, until you come in glory.

Christ has died, Christ is risen, Christ will come again.

John 17: The Priestly Prayer of Jesus

In this chapter John takes us into the mind and heart of Jesus as the hour has come for him to enter his passion and glorification. As the mediator between earth and heaven he is about to exercise his priestly role. Prayer is the fruit of our awareness of God's involvement in all that is happening in life. Here the prayer of Jesus is the expression of
 – his experience of returning to the glory of the Father;
 – his relationship with the disciples;
 – his desire for the unity of later generations of disciples.

The Father's glory
[1]After saying this, Jesus lifted up his eyes to heaven and said, 'Father, the hour has come; give glory to your Son, that the Son may give glory to you, [2]through the power you gave him over all mortals, to bring eternal life to all you have entrusted to him. [3]For this is eternal life: to know you, the only true God, and the One you sent, Jesus Christ.
[4]I have glorified you on earth and finished the work that you gave me to do. [5]Now, Father, give me in your presence the same Glory I had with you before the world began.

The prayer of Jesus firstly manifests his deep relationship with the Father. In John's gospel the constant union of Jesus with the Father is so much emphasised that the focus on the return of Jesus to glory virtually obscures the suffering of his passion and death. Having come in human flesh his divine glory was disguised but now the hour had come for him to be revealed in the light of the Father's glory.

His prayer is not self-centred but he rejoices that the glory of the Father will be reflected in his own glorification. Furthermore the knowledge of divine glory would be extended to 'all that you have entrusted to me', namely his disciples. Eternal life is already being experienced in knowing the Father who had been revealed by Jesus in his mission on earth.

Prayer for the disciples

[6] I have made your name known to the people you gave me from the world. They were yours and you gave them to me, and they kept your word. [7] And now they know that all you have given me comes indeed from you. [8] I have given them the teaching I received from you, and they receive it and know in truth that I came from you; and they believe that you have sent me.

[9] I pray for them; I do not pray for the world but for those who belong to you and whom you have given to me – [10] indeed all I have is yours and all you have is mine – and now they are my glory. [11] I am no longer in the world, but they are in the world whereas I am going to you. Holy Father, keep them in your Name, the Name that you have given me, so that they may be one, just as we are one.

[12] When I was with them, I kept them safe in your Name, and not one was lost except the one who was already lost, and in this the Scripture was fulfilled. [13] But now I am coming to you and I leave my message in the world that my joy may be complete in them.

[14] I have given them your message and the world has hated them because they are not of the world; just as I am not of the world. [15] I do not ask you to remove them from the world but to keep them from the evil one. [16] They shall not be of the world, for I am not of the world.

[17] Consecrate them in the truth – your word is truth – [18] for I have sent them into the world as you sent me into the world. [19] For their sake, I go to the sacrifice by which I am consecrated, so that they too may be consecrated in truth.

Jesus then prays out of his relationship with the disciples. Who are these disciples? They are drawn by the Father and given to Jesus, who passed on divine revelation to them and they accepted it.

The prayer of Jesus in this instance is for those who had accepted his message. Those who belong to the world are those who did not accept him and they are outside the ambit of this particular prayer. It does not mean that they are outside the desire of Jesus that all would be saved and come to a knowledge of the truth.

While Jesus is going to the Father the disciples would still remain in the world with all its trials. But Jesus was going to raise them up by the gift of the Holy Spirit through whom they would receive the power to become children of God, belonging to the Father just like Jesus. His prayer for them is expressed in five petitions:

– that they would remain faithful to their calling, unlike Judas who went his own way;

– that they would be one in the likeness of the union of Father and Son;

– that they would experience divine joy;

– that they be protected from the evil one;

– that they be consecrated or sanctified in the truth, growing more like unto God in holiness through the word that he had given them.

Unity of later disciples

20I pray not only for these but also for those who through their word will believe in me. 21May they all be one as you Father are in me and I am in you. May they be one in us; so the world may believe that you have sent me.
22I have given them the Glory you have given me, that they may be one as we are one. 23I in them and you in me. Thus they shall reach perfection in unity and the world shall know that you have sent me and I have loved them just as you loved me.
24Father, since you have given them to me, I want them to be with me where I am and see the Glory you gave me, for you loved me before the foundation of the world.
25Righteous Father, the world has not known you but I know you, and these have known that you have sent me. 26As I revealed your Name to them, so will I continue to reveal it, so that the love with which you loved me may be in them and I also may be in them.'

Jesus then looks down the future ages to the disciples of later generations. What he prays for especially is for unity in their ranks to reflect on earth the unity in love of the divine persons.

He was going away to prepare a place with the Father for his disciples and now his prayer expresses his desire for their sharing in divine glory. The beatific vision is an eternity of knowing God and being totally united in the love of God. 'As I revealed your Name to them, so will I continue to reveal it, so that the love with which you loved me in them and I also may be in them.' The Father has reached out to embrace us with his two arms: in the visible arm of his revealed Word, Jesus Christ; and with the invisible arm of the Holy Spirit of divine love dwelling in the soul.

Connecting

The upper room where the last supper was held becomes a symbol of prayer. Jesus lifted up his eyes to heaven. The classical definition of prayer is the elevation of the mind and soul to God. Prayer is the threshold between earth and heaven. Our feet are still entrenched in this world but at the threshold of prayer we knock on the door of heaven.

The faithless mind, having had no contact with heaven, would have judged that the programme of Jesus was crashing about him and that all was falling apart. But in prayer, raising his eyes to heaven, Jesus is returning to the centre where, in fact, all is one. There is a serene unity between Father and Son beneath the storms on the surface of life. The divine perspective of Jesus transcends the small-minded plotting of enemies. Nothing, not even betrayal and death, can break the inner core of unity. The trials of death serve to reveal the depth of divine obedience. In this total accomplishment of the Father's will, Jesus manifests his glory.

Jesus prays that his disciples too will share in this inner centre of knowledge and love. The fullness of life is to know the Father, the only true God, by knowing the Son whom he has sent.

We, the disciples of Christ today, remain in the world. When we experience failure or fear, when everything is crashing down around us, then it is time to raise our minds to their upper room and connect with the greater reality. In these days of pressure and depression, of stress and suicide, it is significant that the Holy Spirit has directed many people to centering prayer: that is, the practice of holding the mind on the presence of God at the inner centre of our being. All too easily we let ourselves be submerged by the noise and pace of life. We neglect the inner stillness where one is aware of the divine presence. If we succumb to the bad news then we will not live in the upper room but in the dark basement of fretting and fear.

If you want to spend your life alternating between anxiety and depression simply let the bad news set up squatter's rights in your mind. Join the club of those who have a compulsion to hear the news at every hour in case they miss some scandal or disaster, while in between bulletins they can hear every grievance in the country aired on the phone-in, moan-in programme. Their mental diet each day is a menu of injustices and chicanery, accidents and disasters, gruesome violence and salacious scandals.

In the basement of bad news there is little light and no hope. Like Jesus at the hour of climax we must go to the upper room and stay at the threshold of God in prayer. Prayer brings increasing awareness of a relationship with God. It expands our space and extends our vision of life. It grows in the intimacy of knowing God and Jesus Christ whom he has sent. It wells up from silent depths to eloquence in praise and petition, in thankfulness and contrition. In that upper room we raise our minds and hearts to God and experience the transformation of life.

Praying

Lord Jesus, our Priest and Mediator with the Father. How consoling are your words! How encouraging to hear the inner sentiments of your heart as you prepared to leave this world to return to the Father's glory.

Our great hope is to make that eternal journey to the Father with you. But for the present we remain in this world of struggle, temptation and contradiction. But you have prayed for us.

May we never forget that you have prayed that we would be faithful to your word, sharing in your joy, protected from the evil one and consecrated in the truth.

Lord, you prayed for unity in your flock, now divided into many thousand sections. Your sacred word and Spirit of divine love are the sources of unity. May our misunderstandings be cleared up in the light of your word. May the hurts and prejudices of the past be healed by the outpouring of your Spirit. May the desire for unity replace our complacency. May the third millennium of Christianity be a jubilee of forgiveness, reconciliation and reunification.

John 18-19: The Passing of Jesus

We have recognised the significance of Jewish feasts behind John's writing. Chapters Eighteen and Nineteen are still in the context introduced in John 13:1, before the feast of the Passover, when Jesus knew that the time had come for him to pass from this world to the Father. In this time-setting John writes of the passing of Jesus rather than the passion of Jesus. The emphasis is taken from his human suffering and put on his free control of all that happens, in obedience to the Father and in fulfilment of what had been written, especially in the figure of the Passover lamb.

John omits the anguish of Gethsemane, the need of help from Simon of Cyrene, the consolation from the women of Jerusalem, the hours of darkness and the cry of utter dereliction from the cross. These signs of weakness and dependence are not part of John's picture.

There are several details which suggest the testimony of an eyewitness, such as naming Malchus whose ear was cut off by Simon Peter, the identification of the paved courtyard (Lithostratos) where Pilate sat in judgement, and the charcoal fire where Peter warmed his hands. Indeed, the writer claims the authority of an eyewitness about the pouring of blood and water from the pierced side of Jesus. Yet the main concern of John is the religious meaning of the events. It is the hour of the passing of Jesus to the Father, the inauguration of the new Passover.

Jesus had described his mission in terms of a journey down and up: 'As I came from the Father and have come into the

JOHN 18-19: THE PASSING OF JESUS

world, so I am leaving the world and going to the Father' (Jn 16:28). As the one who has come down from on high he is King and witness to the truth and so he must be shown to be totally free in all that happens. Then as the one lifted up to the Father he is the new Passover Lamb, the one who takes away the sins of the world.

King and witness to truth

[1] When Jesus had finished speaking, he went with his disciples to the other side of the Kidron Valley, a garden was there which Jesus and his disciples entered.

[2] Now Judas, who betrayed him, knew the place since Jesus had often met there with his disciples. [3] He led soldiers of the Roman battalion and guards from the chief priests and Pharisee, who went there with lanterns, torches and weapons.

[4] Jesus knew all that was going to happen to him; he stepped forward and asked, 'Who are you looking for?' [5] They answered, 'Jesus the Nazarene.' Jesus said, 'I am he.' Judas, who betrayed him, stood there with them.

[6] When Jesus said, 'I am he', they moved back and fell to the ground. [7] He then asked a second time, 'Who are you looking for?' and they answered, 'Jesus the Nazarene.' [8] Jesus replied, 'I told you that I am he. If you are looking for me, let these others go.' [9] Thus what Jesus had said came true: 'I have not lost one of those you gave me.'

[10] Simon Peter had a sword; he drew it and struck Malchus, the High Priest's servant, cutting off his right ear. [11] But Jesus said to Peter, 'Put your sword into its sheath; shall I not drink the cup which the Father has given me?'

Kingly Freedom

The royal freedom of Jesus is established from the very beginning. Judas and the soldiers carry torches and weapons for they travel in darkness and in need of protection. But Jesus, the Light, knows everything that is about to happen. When he identifies himself with the divine title, 'I am he', Judas and the soldiers stumble and fall backwards. Jesus is the free one here. Simon Peter draws a sword to offer a violent defence which Jesus refuses. He goes forward freely to drink the cup that the Father has given.

Before Pilate

[12] So the guards and the soldiers, with their commander, seized Jesus and bound him; [13] and they took him first to Annas. Annas was the father-in-law of Caiaphas, who was the High Priest that year; [14] and it was Caiaphas who had told the Jews: 'It is better that one man should die for the people.'

[15] Simon Peter with another disciple followed Jesus. Because this disciple was known to the High Priest, they let him enter the courtyard of the High Priest along with Jesus, [16] but Peter had to stay outside at the door. The other disciple, who was known to the High Priest went out and spoke to the maidservant at the gate and brought Peter in. [17] Then, this servant on duty at the door said to Peter, 'So you also are one of his disciples?' But he answered, 'I am not.'

[18] Now the servants and the guards had made a charcoal fire and were standing and warming themselves because it was cold, and Peter also was with them warming himself.

[19] The High Priest questioned Jesus about his disciples and his teaching. [20] Jesus answered him, 'I have spoken openly to the world; I have always taught in places where the Jews meet together, either at the assemblies in synagogues or in the Temple. I did not teach secretly. [21] Why then do you ask me? Ask those who heard me, they know what I said.'

[22] At this reply one of the guards standing by gave Jesus a blow on the face, saying, 'Is that the way to answer the High Priest?' [23] Jesus said to him, 'If I have spoken wrongly, point it out; but if I have spoken rightly, why do you strike me?'

[24] Then Annas sent him, bound, to Caiaphas, the High Priest.

[25] Now Simon Peter stood there warming himself. They said to him, 'Surely you also are one of his disciples.' He denied it and answered, 'I am not.' [26] But one of the High Priest's servants, a kinsman of the one whose ear Peter had cut off, asked, 'Did I not see you with him in the garden?' [27] Again Peter denied it, and at once the cock crew.

[28] They then led Jesus from the house of Caiaphas to the court of the Roman governor. It was now morning. The Jews didn't enter lest they be made unclean (by coming into the house of a pagan) and be unable to eat the Passover meal. [29] So Pilate went out and asked, 'What charge do you bring against this man?'

They answered, [30] If he were not a criminal, we would not be handing him over to you.' [31] Pilate said, 'Take him yourselves and judge him according to your own law.' But they replied, 'We ourselves are not allowed to put anyone to death.'

JOHN 18-19: THE PASSING OF JESUS

³²It was clear from this what kind of death Jesus was to die, according to what Jesus himself had foretold.
³³Pilate then entered the court again, called Jesus and asked him,'Are you the King of the Jews?' ³⁴Jesus replied, 'Are you saying this of your own accord, or did other say it to you?'
³⁵Pilate answered, 'Am I a Jew? Your own nation and the chief priests have handed you over to me. What have you done?' ³⁶Jesus answered, 'My kingship does not come from this world. If I were king like those of this world, my guards would have fought to save me from being handed over to the Jews. But my kingship is not from here.'
³⁷Pilate asked him, 'So you are a king?' And Jesus answered, 'Just as you say, I am a king. For this I was born and for this I have come into the world, to bear witness to the truth. Everyone who is one the side of truth hears my voice.' ³⁸Pilate said, 'What is truth?'
Pilate then went out to the Jews again and said, 'I find no crime in this man. ³⁹Now, according to a custom, I must release a prisoner of yours at the Passover. With your agreement I will release for you the King of the Jews.' ⁴⁰But, they insisted and cried out, 'Not this man, but Barabbas!' Now Barabbas was a robber.

19 ¹Then Pilate had Jesus taken away and scourged. ²The soldiers also twisted thorns into a crown and put it on his head. They threw a cloak of royal purple around his shoulders ³and began coming up to him and saluting him, 'Hail, king of the Jews', and they struck him on the face.
⁴Pilate went outside yet another time and said to the Jews, 'Look, I am bringing him out and I want you to know that I find no crime in him.' ⁵Jesus then came out wearing the crown of thorns and the purple cloak and Pilate pointed to him saying, 'Here is the man!'
⁶On seeing him the chief priests and the guards cried out, 'Crucify him! Crucify him!' Pilate replied 'Take him yourselves and have him crucified, for I find no case against him.' ⁷The Jews then said, 'We have a Law, and according to the Law this man must die because he made himself Son of God.'
⁸When Pilate heard this he was more afraid. ⁹And coming back into the court he asked Jesus, 'Where are you from?' But Jesus gave him no answer. ¹⁰Then Pilate said to him, 'You will not speak to me? Do you not know that I have power to release you just as I have power to crucify you?' ¹¹Jesus replied, 'You would have no power over me unless it had been given you from above; therefore the one who handed me over to you is even more guilty.'
¹²Because of this Pilate tried to release him, but the Jews cried out,

'If you release this man, you are not a friend of Caesar. Anyone who makes himself king is defying Caesar.'
¹³When Pilate heard this, he had Jesus brought outside to the place called the Stone Floor – in Hebrew Gabbatha – and there he seated him in the judge's seat. ¹⁴It was the Preparation Day for the Passover, about noon. So Pilate said to the Jews, 'Here is your king.' ¹⁵But they cried out, 'Away! Take him away! Crucify him!' Pilate replied, 'Shall I crucify your king?' And the chief priests answered, 'We have no king but Caesar.'
¹⁶Then Pilate handed Jesus over to them to be crucified, and they took charge of him.

John makes no mention of the trial before the Jewish Sanhedrin, nor of the charges relating to destroying the temple. These matters have been adequately dealt with already in this gospel. There is a short account of the questioning of Jesus before Annas and Caiaphas. In the courtyard outside Peter went to warm himself at the charcoal fire and there occurred his threefold denial of acquaintance with Jesus.

The trial before Pilate is related at length in carefully constructed detail. There are seven episodes located alternately outside and inside the Pretorium. The fourth and central episode is the key to the chiastic construction. This is when Jesus is crowned and mocked as King of the Jews. John places the royal title in this central position in order to highlight the issue of kingship. The irony of the mock crowning is that Jesus is in fact the King.

Irony recurs in the unfolding of the story. The Jews would not go inside the house of the foreigner, Pilate, lest they be defiled and unable to eat the Passover meal, not realising that the one whose death they were seeking would be the new Passover Lamb.

Pilate respects military authority and appreciates political bargaining, but he is cynical about truth which to him is expendable. Jesus represents truth and his kingdom is not about power but about truth. For this had he come into the world, to witness to the truth. The truth which is in Jesus makes him totally free whereas Pilate, for all his seeming power, is not free. Jesus tells him that he would have no power had it not been given to him from above. There is a double meaning here because above can mean from God or from the higher Roman authorities. Indeed, the Jewish accusers refer to their contact with Caesar as a form of blackmail to trap Pilate.

The chief priests themselves lose their freedom as they become so trapped in political intrigue that they tell Pilate: 'We have no king but Caesar.' This is utter heresy for a Jew, the denial of their unique identity as the nation covenanted to God. Pilate enjoys his moment of revenge in ordering the sign 'Jesus the Nazorean, King of the Jews' to be displayed in Hebrew, Latin and Greek, making a universal declaration.

The Dying Moments

[17]Bearing his own cross, Jesus went out of the city to what is called the Place of the Skull, in Hebrew: Golgotha. [18]There he was crucified and with him two others, one one either side and Jesus was in the middle.

[19]Pilate had a notice written and fastened to the cross that read: Jesus the Nazorean, King of the Jews. [20]Many Jewish people saw this title because the place where Jesus was crucified was very close to the city. It was, moreover, written in Hebrew, Latin and Greek. [21]The chief priests said to Pilate, 'Do not write: "The king of the Jews"; but: This man claimed to be king of the Jews.' [22]Pilate answered them, 'What I have written, I have written.'

[23]When the soldiers crucified Jesus, they took his clothes and divided them into four parts, one part for each of them. But as for the tunic it was woven in one piece from top to bottom, [24]so they said, 'Let us not tear it, but cast lots to decide who will get it.' This fulfilled the words of Scripture: They divided my clothing among themselves; they cast lost for my garment. And this was what the soldiers did.

[25]Near the cross of Jesus stood his mother, his mother's sister Mary, who was the wife of Cleophas, and Mary of Magdala. [26]When Jesus saw the Mother, and the disciple, he said to the Mother, 'Woman, this is your son.' [27]Then he said to the disciple, 'There is your mother.' And from that moment the disciple took her to his own home.

[28]After that Jesus knew that all was now finished and he said, 'I am thirsty' as it was written in Scripture. [29]A jar full of bitter wine stood there; so, putting a sponge soaked in the wine on a hyssop stalk,

they raised it to his lips. ³⁰Jesus took the wine and said, 'It is accomplished.' Then he bowed his head and gave up the spirit.

³¹As it was Preparation Day, the Jews did not want the bodies to remain on the cross during the sabbath, as this sabbath was a very solemn day. So they asked Pilate to have the legs of the condemned men broken, so they might take away the bodies.

³²The soldiers came and broke the legs of the first man and of the other who had been crucified with Jesus. ³³When they came to Jesus, they saw that he was already dead; so they did not break his legs. ³⁴One of the soldiers, however, pierced his side with a lance and immediately there came out blood and water.

³⁵This is the testimony given by one who saw it; his testimony is true and Another knows that he speaks the truth. This man gives his witness so that you may believe as well. ³⁶All this happened to fulfill the words of Scripture, Not one of his bones shall be broken. ³⁷Another text says: They shall look on him whom they have pierced.

³⁸After this, Joseph of Arimathea approached Pilate, for he was a disciple of Jesus, although secretly, for fear of the Jews. And he asked Pilate to let him remove the body of Jesus. And Pilate agreed. So, he came and took away the body.

³⁹Nicodemus, the man who earlier had come to Jesus by night, also came and brought a jar of myrrh mixed with aloes, about a hundred pounds. ⁴⁰They took the body of Jesus and wrapped it in linen cloths with the spices, following the burial custom of the Jews.

⁴¹There was a garden in the place where Jesus had been crucified, and, in the garden, a new tomb in which no one had ever been laid.⁴² As the tomb was very near, they buried Jesus there because they had no time left before the Jewish Preparation Day.

Even on the cross Jesus remains in control of all that is happening. His seamless garment is not torn, symbolic of his flock which is to be one and undivided. He makes provision for the care of his mother. The mother of Jesus and the beloved disciple are not named, probably an invitation to see them both, not merely as individuals but, as representative people. Jesus knowingly fulfils the words of scripture, 'I am thirsty'. Even the moment of death is described as the free choice of Jesus. 'It is accomplished', he announces. Then bowing his head he gives up his spirit or breath.

Death on the cross normally came when the lungs of the victim could no longer function as the head and chest increasingly pressed down on the diaphragm. John has depicted Jesus as freely deciding when to bow his head and when to return his final breath (spirit) to the Father from whom the breath of life is on loan. Throughout John's account, then, Jesus is free, noble and kingly until the very end.

Jesus, the Passover Lamb

If Jesus as King is God bending down to our human condition, then Jesus as the new Passover Lamb represents humanity rising to God in sacrifice.

At the beginning of his ministry, John the Baptist identified Jesus as the Lamb of God who takes away the sins of the world. The theme of the sacrificial lamb is woven into the text. The sentencing of Jesus to death took place about the sixth hour, midday, on the Passover Preparation Day. John is making the point that the crucifixion of Jesus occurred at the time when the lambs were being ritually slaughtered in the temple.

The sponge dipped in sour wine was held to the lips of Jesus on a hyssop plant. Hyssop is a pliant fern, hardly suitable for holding up a sponge, but it links the story with the hyssop used at the original Passover to sprinkle the blood of sacrificed lambs on the doorposts of the Hebrews in Egypt to save them from the destroying angel.

The legs of Jesus were not broken by the soldiers, another link with the Passover lamb, not one of whose bones should be broken. The blood and water flowing from the pierced side of Jesus is the blood of sacrifice and the water of new life.

Connecting

John's story invites us to look at the events and meditate on their significance. It is the hour when Jesus is lifted up from the earth, drawing all people to himself. He is the true King who came down from on high now returning to the Father. He is the Passover Lamb in whose blood our lives are saved from the slave-land of sin.

'They shall look on him whom they have pierced.' As we see the flow of water from his side we recall the many uses of water in this gospel: the water of purification changed into the wine of marriage celebration at Cana: the water of new life in the Spirit, as explained to Nicodemus: the inner springs of eternal satisfaction promised to the woman at the well: the healing waters of Siloam: the Exodus water gushing from the rock foreshadowing the rivers of life flowing from the heart of believers in the days of the Spirit. In baptism we are reborn in the sanctifying waters of the Spirit.

Looking at the pierced side of the Lord we also see the flow of blood: the passover blood sealing the new covenant: the blood of the lamb guarding our houses from destruction: the blood of the Lord's living presence in the Eucharist ... the Lord abiding in us and we in the Lord ... pulsing in our hearts and flowing in our veins as the sustenance of Christian energy.

Praying

We adore you, O Christ, and we bless you because by your holy cross you have redeemed the world.

Jesus, Lamb of God who takes away the sins of the world, have mercy on us.

Lord Jesus, your cross lifted up before our eyes is a book in which we read many lessons. There we see your love. Having loved us in your coming down from above, you loved us to the end. No greater love could you have shown than by laying down your life for us.

On the cross we see the ugliness of sin in the wounds inflicted on your body: the tearing of thorns on your head for all sins of the mind: the lacerations of whips on your body for all sins of the flesh: the pierced hands for sins of clenched fists and weapons of violence: the wounded feet for sins of straying from your way: your pierced heart for all who betray your love.

The next lesson we read on the cross is hope. For it is by your wounds that we are healed. And you are the Lamb of God who takes away the sins of the world.

On the cross you teach the lesson of how to suffer without bitterness, how to endure injustice without retaliation.

Let us look on the one they have pierced.

Let us rejoice in the new life of baptism symbolised in the water flowing from your side.

Let us draw the energy for Christian living from the chalice of your sacred blood flowing from your heart.

John 20: The Empty Tomb

¹Now, on the first day after the sabbath, Mary of Magdala came to the tomb early in the morning, while it was still dark and she saw that the stone blocking the tomb had been moved away. ²So she ran to Peter and the other disciple whom Jesus loved. And she said to them, 'They have taken the Lord out of the tomb and we don't know where they have laid him.'
³Peter then set out with the other disciple to go to the tomb. ⁴They ran together but the other disciple outran Peter and reached the tomb first. ⁵He bent down and saw the linen cloths lying flat, but he did not enter.
⁶Then Simon Peter came following him and entered the tomb; he too, saw the linen cloths lying flat. ⁷The napkin, which had been put around his head was not lying flat like the other linen cloths but it stayed rolled up in its place. ⁸Then the other disciple who had reached the tomb first also went in; he saw and believed. ⁹For as yet they did not know that the Scriptures foretold his rising from the dead.
¹⁰After that the disciples went home again.

Nowhere in scripture is there an account of the actual moment of resurrection. What the gospels give are two types of story: first, accounts of finding that the tomb was empty; and then, stories about encounters of the risen Lord with various disciples. Each story dramatises some aspect of how Christians continue to meet with the Lord and respond to him in faith.

The first day of the week suggests the beginning of the new age of resurrection time after the period of the enfleshed life of Jesus on earth. But it was still dark for the disciples had not yet arrived at the light of faith in the resurrection.

The large stone had been moved away from the tomb. The evangelist injects a note of excitement into the narrative in describ-

JOHN 20: THE EMPTY TOMB

ing how Mary of Magdala ran to Peter and the beloved disciple. But she did not venture beyond saying 'They have taken the Lord out of the tomb and we don't know where they have put him.'

The two apostles, likewise, ran to the tomb, the younger one getting there before Peter but he deferred to the authority or seniority of Peter by letting him enter first. Peter verified that the tomb was indeed empty and he noted the position of the various binding cloths. Yet these material facts did not enable him to make the step of faith in the resurrection. The disciple who personified the love of the Lord made that step of faith: he saw and he believed. In that moment of light all darkness was banished as they understood what the scriptures had said that he must rise from the dead.

Connecting

When we were young, Lent meant giving up sweets. No big deal really because sweets were not too plentiful. What few we got were hoarded in carefully hidden jamjars. We saved up for a binge of sweetness at Easter. The Russian Orthodox, in some places, had the tradition of saving their jokes during Lent to make Easter day a binge of hilarity. Their reasoning was that Easter was the greatest practical joke of all time. Just when Satan was about to mount the victory podium the mat was pulled from underneath him. The tomb was empty! It was the first day of the week.

The essence of humour is in the unexpected twist, the little oddity, something incongruous, the tumbling of the mighty. And how we need a sense of the divine humour to survive this deadly serious season of scandals, surveys and statistics.

That there are faults and sins in the church nobody can deny. But there's another part of the divine joke. That God should have chosen such frail men and women to be the dispensers of the sacred mysteries!

Surveys and statistics remind me of Peter, the original detective, inspecting the linen cloths on the ground and noting that the other cloth, used as a headpiece, was in a different place. A dossier of facts and measurements brought him no nearer to faith. It was the disciple who personified the love of the Lord who saw the light and believed.

Easter is the renewed call from God to come out of the dark tombs of death and doubt, of failure and guilt, of anxiety and distrust. The power of God's angels will roll back the boulders. Why look among the dead for one who is alive?

It is said that the student of scripture has to be scholar, artist and mystic. Scholar to understand the text: artist to play creatively with the words and see the link with the world of today: and mystic to recognise the presence of the Lord. It takes an angelic sense of humour to mix them all together. One needs to take on board the incongruity of the incarnation, the paradox of the cross, the weeds and wheat nature of the church. And even then, the intelligence of the fallen angels was taken for a ride until the dawning light of that first day revealed an empty tomb.

Praying

Risen Lord Jesus, we adore you.

With you it is always a new day and a time of light.

Send your holy angels to roll back the heavy stones that lock us into tombs of grief and sadness, caves of darkness and despair.

Send your Holy Spirit to take out of our flesh the hearts of stone and give us hearts of flesh, hearts that are full of love, your love. For it is love alone that will recognise your presence, as it did for the beloved disciple.

Risen Lord, with you every day is an Easter, a day of rising and renewal.

Encounters with the Risen Lord

It is important to distinguish between resuscitation and resurrection. Resuscitation is what Lazarus experienced. It means coming back in the old form of life. Resurrection is not a coming back but a going forward to a new life, transformed and glorious.

JOHN 20: THE EMPTY TOMB 151

For the sake of the visionaries the glory of the Lord was sifted to the limits of their senses. He became accessible to sight, hearing and touch: he cooked food and ate it.

The encounters of the risen Lord with the various disciples represent different ways in which Christians of all times continue to meet the Lord in their lives. These are stories of faith, answering the question, 'Where is the Lord to be found?'

In each story there are three vital stages:
- the description of the fear and confusion beforehand;
- the dramatic moment of recognition;
- the message and mission given to the visionary.

Encounter with Mary of Magdala

¹¹Mary stood weeping outside the tomb and as she wept, she bent down to look inside; ¹²and she saw two angels in white sitting where the body of Jesus had been, one at the head, and the other at the feet. ¹³They said, 'Woman, why are you weeping?' She answered, 'Because they have taken my Lord and I don't know where they have put him.'

¹⁴As she said this, she turned around and saw Jesus standing there but she did not recognize him. ¹⁵Jesus said to her, 'Woman, why are you weeping? Who are you looking for?' She thought it was the gardener and answered him, 'If you have taken him away, tell me where you have put him, and I will go and remove him.' ¹⁶Jesus said to her, 'Mary'. She turned and said to him, 'Rabboni' – which means Master. ¹⁷Jesus said to her, 'Do not hold on to me; you see I have not yet ascended to the Father. But go to my brothers and say to them: I am ascending to my Father, who is your Father, to my God, who is your God.'

¹⁸So Mary of Magdala went and said to the disciples, 'I have seen the Lord, and this is what he said to me.'

Mary of Magdala was one of the faithful followers who stood by the cross of Jesus as he died (Jn 19:25). It was she who brought the news of the empty tomb to the apostles but she had not yet received the light of faith in the resurrection. Her distress is depicted in the picture of her standing, outside the tomb, weeping. But at least she was searching.

The angels in white, sitting where the body of Jesus had been, represent the linking of heaven and earth once promised to Nathanael (Jn 1:51). It seems extraordinary that Mary showed no great reaction to the vision of angels. Nothing less than her Lord and Master would satisfy her search.

The repeated complaint of Mary that someone, possibly the gardener, had taken away the body may be an editorial touch added by the evangelist to answer people of his own day who were making that claim.

When the Lord appeared to her she did not recognise him on the physical level of sight or sound of familiar voice. Recognition came when she heard herself called by name, 'Mary!' This is the moment when everything changes. She responded, 'Rabboni!', a title higher than Rabbi, probably an act of faith. The instruction of the Lord to her contains two important missionary messages.

1. 'Do not hold on to me.' If, in the days before Calvary, relationships with Jesus involved physical recognition, this was no longer the case. Jesus was now in the process of ascending to the Father.

2. She is to bring the message to the brothers, 'I am ascending to my Father, who is your Father, to my God, who is your God.' Jesus had promised that when he was lifted up he would draw all people to himself (Jn 12:32). All who accepted him would receive the power to become children of God (1:12). The Lord would be their divine brother. His Father would be their Father too.

Where is the risen Lord encountered? This story dramatises the experience of personal call and the message that whoever is one with Christ Jesus is a child of God the Father.

Connecting

Where do we hear the personal call of the Lord in our lives? What prevents us from recognising his presence? The Easter story of Magdalene illustrates aspects of how the Lord reveals himself to us. In each encounter story we can connect with the confused state before the Lord's coming. Then comes the moment of recognition and finally the missionary message.

JOHN 20: THE EMPTY TOMB

Three words paint the stark picture of Magdalene's confusion – standing, outside, weeping.

Standing – staying put, she was not moving from the days of the old contact with Jesus to the new age of the risen Lord. She wanted to cling to the past, physical reality, rather than embrace the new mode of existence.

Outside – she had not entered the realm of faith. It is reminiscent of the famous passage in the Confessions of Saint Augustine.

> Late have I loved you, beauty so old and so new: late have I loved you. And see, you were within and I was in the external world and sought you there, and in my unlovely state I plunged into those lovely creatures which you made. You were with me and I was not with you. These lovely things kept me from you, though if they did not have their existence in you, they had no existence at all ...

(Saint Augustine: *Confessions*, translator Chadwick, O.U.P, 1991, p. 201).

Weeping – she resembled Mary of Bethany whose faith was obscured by grief at the death of her brother, Lazarus.

The key to understanding any of these encounter stories is the manner in which the Lord makes his presence known. On the Emmaus road it was at the breaking of the bread that their eyes were opened and they recognised him. For Magdalene the moment of recognition comes when the Lord calls her by name, 'Mary!'. The Lord is the Good Shepherd who knows his flock and calls each one by name.

The soliloquy of Augustine continues with a description of his call, a profound experience involving all the senses.

> You called and cried out loud and shattered my deafness. You were radiant and resplendent, you put to flight my blindness. You were fragrant, and I drew in my breath and now pant after you. I tasted you, and I feel but hunger and thirst for you. You touched me, and I am set on fire to attain the peace which is yours.

The missionary message given to Mary is that the old way of relating to Jesus on the physical level has been transformed into a new and more wonderful relationship in which the disciple is raised to unity with Christ in divine adoption. The God and Father of Jesus Christ is our God and Father too.

Where do we meet the Lord today? This episode tells us that one path of faith is in hearing the voice of God who loves me and calls me by name.

I have called you by your name, you are mine (Is 43:1).

This story of faith can be connected with the call to celibacy in priestly life. A celibate vocation is the experience of a personal call from God. It is a call to a relationship not of a physical nature ... 'do not cling to me thus'... but of personal brotherhood with Jesus. It is a call to witness to the risen Lord and to the new relationship of being children of God the Father. A life of consecrated celibacy is an anticipation of the union of heaven where there is neither marriage nor giving in marriage.

Praying

Risen Lord, you have called me by name. I am yours.

You call me to life and faith each new day. Yet so often I stay on the outside, so caught up in my personal agenda that I do not see you or hear you. Even when you send me angels of light I fail to be moved by them.

Grant me, Lord, the fullness of your Spirit in a lively faith.

Strengthen my resolve to spend time with you each day.

As a child looks into it's mother's eyes with a smile of recognition and gratitude, so may I look at you many times every day.

Lift me up from the weakness of sin to a life of union with you.

Help me to appreciate the immense privilege of being a child of God.

Grant that I might know what it means to call God Our Father.

JOHN 20: THE EMPTY TOMB

Behind Closed Doors

[19] On the evening of that day, the first day after the sabbath, the doors were locked where the disciples were, because of their fear of the Jews, but Jesus came and stood among them. He said to them, 'Peace be with you;' [20] then he showed them his hands and his side. The disciples kept looking at the Lord and were full of joy. [21] Again Jesus said to them, 'Peace be with you. As the Father has sent me, so I am sending you.' [22] After saying this he breathed on them and said to them, 'Receive the Holy Spirit; [23] for those whose sins you forgive, they are forgiven; for those whose sins you retain, they are retained.'

The images of gathering darkness and closed doors accentuate the mood of fear before the presence of the Lord is recognised. The closed doors, in a sense, contradict the message of the stone rolled back from the tomb. Then Jesus came and stood among them. His very presence exudes Shalom, that peace he had promised them beyond anything the world could offer.

The manner of recognition is in showing them his wounded hands and side. Then the Lord explained their mission. 'As the Father sent me,' this was the first mission: now he was announcing the commencement of the second mission ... 'so I am sending you.'

Jesus had announced the completion of his own mission on Calvary: 'It is accomplished'. After saying this 'he bowed his head and gave up the spirit' (19:30). His physical body which had been the vehicle of his mission on earth no longer needed the breath of life. In biblical thought, life, signified by breath, was on loan from the Creator and was returned to God in dying.

You send forth your spirit and they are created.

You take back your spirit and they die,

returning to the dust from which they came (Ps 103).

The breath which Jesus returned to the Father is now bestowed on the disciples as he breathed on them and said to them, 'Receive the Holy Spirit ...'

In his own mission Jesus was identified as the Lamb of God who takes away the sins of the world. And in several places he denounced the sin of those who refused to believe. For instance, after the healing of the blind man he told the Pharisees, 'Your guilt remains' (9:41). The disciples are now empowered by the Spirit for the same double mission of forgiving the repented sin and denouncing or retaining the unrepented sin.

Connecting

The key to connecting with the encounter is to be found in the moment of recognition, the invitation of the Lord to look at his wounded hands and side. It might seem an unlikely place to encounter the divine presence but it is a story that is daily repeated in the wounded members of Christ on earth.

Switching on the radio one afternoon I picked up the fascinating story of the religious conversion of Cecil Hurwitz. A Jewish boy in Cork, he attended a school run by the Presentation Brothers. He left the classroom each day during religious instruction and stayed in the cloakroom where he was expected to study. One day he noticed a small book on the floor which he took to hand and began to read. It was a gospel. An extraordinary experience overtook him when he came to the place where Jesus was nailed to the cross. He, there and then, knelt down, wept for what was done to Jesus and made his first act of Christian faith, 'Lord, I believe.'

Two things struck me as I listened. First, that he knelt down, which would not have been a familiar posture of prayer for a Jew. It must have been an instinctive gesture of humiliation and adoration.

The second point that struck me was the moment of his act of faith. It was not at reading any of the stupendous miracles or great teaching of Jesus, but at his unjust wounding. As with the disciples in the gathering darkness of that first Easter day, faith came for Cecil Hurwitz on beholding the wounds of Jesus.

Mother Teresa's faith leaped into a blazing furnace when she encountered Jesus in the bodies of the destitute. Jean Vanier's faith sees the Christian dignity of the mentally handicapped. Archbishop Oscar Romero was transformed from a timid, upper-class priest into a fiery prophet, who defied an unjust regime, when he met Christ in the injustices suffered by the poor.

JOHN 20: THE EMPTY TOMB

Where is the risen Lord to be found? Our faith tells us that the Lord can be met anywhere. But this gospel encounter suggests that we should pay special attention to the presence of Christ in his brothers and sisters who are wounded by sin and by injustice, discrimination or poverty. The power of the Holy Spirit is met in the mission of the church to heal the wounds of sin and to denounce the injustices and wrongs of society.

Praying

O risen Lord, grant us the grace to know
– that there is no closed door where you cannot enter;
– that there is no fear which cannot be transformed by your peace;
– that there is no repented sin which your forgiveness will not heal.

Open our eyes to see your wounds in the world around us,
– in the victims of injustice or betrayal;
– in all who are handicapped in mind or body;
– in those who are locked behind doors of fear because of their experiences.

O Lord, we thank you for the gift of your Spirit to the church.

May we appreciate the gift of divine reconciliation celebrated in the sacrament.

May we have the courage to denounce the wrongness of sin in ourselves and in others.

O risen Lord, come through our closed doors.

Breathe your Spirit over us.

Thomas

[24] Thomas, the Twin, one of the Twelve, was not with them when Jesus came. [25] The other disciples told him, 'We have seen the Lord.' But he replied, 'Until I have seen in his hands the print of the nails, and put my finger in the mark of the nails and my hand in his side, I will not believe.'

[26] Eight days later, the disciples were in the house again and Thomas was with them. Despite the locked doors Jesus came in. He stood among them and said, 'Peace be with you.' [27] Then he said to Thomas,

'Put your finger here and see my hands; stretch out your hand and put it into my side. Doubt no longer but believe.'
[28]Thomas then said, 'You are my Lord and my God'. [29]Jesus replied, 'You believe because you see me, don't you? Happy are those who believe although they do not see.'

'Eight days later', the following Sunday, it was the end of one week and the beginning of another. The encounter of Thomas with the Lord marks the end of physical contact with the Lord and the beginning of contact through faith without seeing.

Thomas has been met twice before in this gospel. When news came of the illness of Lazarus and Jesus announced that he was going to Judea despite the plans to kill him, all Thomas could foresee was certain death for all of them. Yet his loyalty was unflinching. 'Let us also go that we may die with him' (11:16).

Then at the last supper Thomas said to Jesus, 'Lord, we don't know where you are going: how can we know the way?' (14:5). These two vignettes offer strong hints about his character. People familiar with the Enneagram will see him as the classical Enneagram Six. He senses danger, struggles with fear but will be loyal to a fault. He cannot act on blind instinct nor for the sake of joining the gang but he needs personal proof. Caution and loyalty are to be found together in this character: slow to join a cause but slower still to desert it. A misguided loyalty to Jesus as he had known him kept Thomas back in the old days of physical presence. His doors were stubbornly closed until the risen Lord personally invited him beyond physical contact into the new era of faith.

Recognition and Change

For Thomas, recognition of the Lord came at the invitation to touch the wounds in his hands and side. 'Put your finger here and see my hands; stretch out your hand and put it into my side. Doubt no longer but believe.' The wound in the side of Jesus is the entry into his heart. In this gospel, where signs are so important, the exterior action points to the interior effect. The exterior touch is a sign of the interior touching of the heart of Thomas by the Holy Spirit enabling him to believe. To believe is to give one's mind and heart, *cor dare, credere,* in Latin.

Thomas is changed. He steps out of the past where his misguided loyalty had detained him and he steps into the new era of faith. He makes the highest act of faith in Christ of anybody in the gospel: 'My Lord and my God.' Blessed is Thomas who can see and touch the Lord, but how much greater is the blessing of that interior touch of the heart by which the Holy Spirit enables one to believe.

Connecting

Thomas was called the Twin, as in 11:16. Are we to read significance into this name? Throughout this book, whenever John left a person unnamed we have taken that person as a representative of others.

Perhaps we may regard the pairing of twins as representing the harmony of opposites in each person. Each of us is a mixture of light and shadow, of developed talents and underdeveloped potential, of positive energy and negative diminishments.

All things go in pairs, by opposites,
he has never made anything imperfect:
one thing complements the excellence of another.
Who could ever grow weary of gazing at his glory?
(Sir 42:24-26).

Thomas had to reach into his own twin or shadow side out of which came his stubborn refusal to believe the word of his fellow disciples. Our negative side will erect obstacles in our journey to God. In Thomas, fear, masquerading as loyalty, was at the root of his refusal. Others may be held back by anger, guilt, resentment, envy, intolerance or hurt. Sometimes it is a very thin thread which holds back the flight of a bird.

We can see an instance in the interior conversion of Francis of Assisi. He had begun to take God's call seriously when one day he was faced by a leper on the road. Being a person of highly refined senses, the nauseating stench of rotting flesh would have sickened Francis more than most others, so he spurred his horse to hurry by. But his conscience quickly stopped him. He turned back to the leper, gave him money and embraced him. The moment of embrace changed his life at a very deep level. At that moment, not only did Francis embrace the actual leper but he also embraced the leprous negativity of his own character. In so doing he also embraced the wounded Christ who bore the leprosy of sin. A few days later, Francis experienced the voice of the crucified one clarifying his vocation: 'Francis, repair my church which is falling into ruin.'

Year later, in his last testament, Francis wrote of his feelings that day with the leper. 'What before seemed bitter was changed into sweetness of soul and body.' As in the story of Thomas, the external act of touching the leper brought about the deep, interior touch of the Holy Spirit which transformed his life.

Normally, people deal with negative emotions either by fight of by flight. Fight is shown in resentment, aggressive behaviour or anger. Flight is the way of denial, spurring the horse to escape, or paralysis of action in the PLOM syndrome we saw in the crippled man at the pool. We might bury ourselves in work, or busyness or diversion of any sort. But there is a third option. With the grace of the Holy Spirit we are invited to touch the wound, to negotiate with the negative area: to accept the fact of its existence but to believe that God's grace is there to help one grow in the situation. With God's grace, our problems become possibilities.

I have been privileged to accompany members of Alcoholics Anonymous on the fourth and fifth stages of their journey as they make a very honest moral inventory of their lives and admit the exact nature of their wrongs to God, to themselves and to another human being. They tell of their decision renewed every day, and several times on difficult days, to turn their lives over to the care of God. Not only their drinking but also their thinking has to be healed. They have to probe with total honesty in all areas of insecurity, fear, anger, resentment, inhibitions and non-acceptance of others. It is the truth that makes us free.

I have met men and women who were once broken but have

now attained a very deep life of union with Jesus. They know that they would never have experienced this spiritual life unless they had been broken and powerless. Each time I hear it, I remember how Thomas encountered the risen Lord through the invitation to touch his wounds.

One of the most moving passages in the letters of Saint Paul is where he writes of 'a thorn in my flesh, a true messenger of Satan, to slap me in the face'. Three times he prayed to the Lord to remove the problem, but he answered, 'My grace is enough for you; my great strength is revealed in weakness' (2 Cor 12: 7-9).

Where is the risen Lord to be found? Surprise, surprise! The Lord is met when, in total honesty, we touch our own wounds, limitations and negativity. His power finds room to work in our emptiness. Facing the truth is the way to freedom.

Praying

O risen Lord, come through the closed doors of all who have lost their hope and joy: who can no longer trust others: whose hearts have been deeply wounded.

You drew the hand of Thomas towards your heart that he might be able to get in touch with his own heart.

With your grace break through our stubborn wills and false loyalties. May we let go of our fears and failures, our inhibitions and anxieties. Your great grace is enough for us.

Lord, I believe in you and in your grace.

May my emptiness be a space for the free working of your grace.

May we recognise your special presence in our weakness and brokenness.

Your presence drives out all fear and brings us peace.

You bring us your divine power and new hope.

John 21: Breakfast on the Shore

[1]After this Jesus revealed himself to the disciples by the Lake of Tiberias. He appeared to them in this way. [2]Simon Peter, Thomas who was called the Twin, Nathanael of Cana in Galilee, the sons of Zebedee and two other disciples were together; [3]and Simon Peter said to them, 'I am going to fish.' They replied, 'We will come with you' and they went out and got into the boat. But they caught nothing that night.
[4]When day had already broken, Jesus was standing on the shore, but the disciples did not know that it was Jesus. [5]Jesus called them, 'Children, have you anything to eat?' They answered, 'Nothing.' [6]Then he said to them, 'Throw the net on the right side of the boat and you will find some.' When they had lowered the net, they were not able to pull it in because of the great number of fish.
[7]Then the disciple Jesus loved said to Peter, 'It is the Lord!' At these words, 'It is the Lord', Simon Peter put on his clothes, for he was stripped for work, and jumped into the water. [8]The other disciples came in the boat dragging the net full of fish; they were not far from land, about a hundred meters.
[9]When they landed, they saw a charcoal fire there with fish on it, and some bread. [10]Jesus said to them, 'Bring some of the fish you have just caught.' [11]So Simon Peter climbed into the boat and pulled the net to shore. It was full of big fish – one hundred and fifty-three – but in spite of this, the net was not torn.
[12]Jesus said to them, 'Come and have breakfast,' and not one of the disciples dared ask him, 'Who are you?' for they knew it was the Lord. [13]Jesus then came and took the bread and gave it to them, and he did the same with the fish.
[14]This was the third time that Jesus revealed himself to his disciples after rising from the dead.

The gospel originally ended with Chapter 20:30-31, verses we will look at in the epilogue. Some commentators suggest that

JOHN 21: BREAKFAST ON THE SHORE

this last chapter was added as a corrective for the members of the evangelist's local church community. While they were greatly blessed in having the memories of the beloved disciple, yet they need a reminder of the universal mission of the apostles and, in particular, of the special pastoral role assigned to Peter.

It was by the Sea of Tiberias. Instead of the usual name, Sea of Galilee, the author chooses the Roman name for the lake. It establishes a link with the miracle of the loaves and fishes in Chapter Six, where the gospel uses both names for the lake. The use of the Roman name also opens up the connection with Rome, scene of the mission and death of Peter.

Among the seven fishing was Nathanael, the one to whom Jesus spoke about the great linking up of heaven and earth. This connection with the first chapter rounds off the unity of the gospel.

The setting in the light of morning is an indication that this is the new age of resurrection time. That there were still dark areas in the faith of the apostles is suggested by their going back to the fishing nets and by the fact that they laboured all through the night and caught nothing.

The did not recognise the Lord by sight nor by the sound of his voice. The moment of recognition came at the size of the catch of fish, probably triggering off the memory of another miraculous catch. Once again it is the beloved disciple who makes the recognition: 'It's the Lord!'

The moment of recognition is the key to understanding these post-resurrection encounters. In this instance the catch of fish is a symbol of the mission of the disciples. 'Do not be afraid. From now on it is people you will catch' (Lk 5:10). In this episode we can pick out four important features of the church's mission.

1. As long as the apostles laboured through the night they caught nothing. But once they heard the word of the Lord giving them direction, the catch was huge. The mission of the church is a combination of divine direction and human effort.

2. The nets were not torn, just as the cloak of Jesus was not torn on Calvary. Being untorn expresses the unity of the flock for which Jesus prayed (Jn 17:23).

3. The prominence of Peter in this episode indicates his special authority in the church. He is clearly acting as the captain of the whole operation.

4. The number of fish, one hundred and fifty-three is very significant. Down the centuries commentators have offered various interpretations of the number. Saint Jerome suggested that it corresponds to the number of species of fish, hence indicating a mission to all nations. Saint Cyril of Alexandria, who was very fond of allegorical interpretations, wrote that there were a hundred to represent the Gentile nations of the world, fifty for the Jewish remnant and three in honour of the Blessed Trinity.

The total number, one hundred and fifty-three, is the combined total of all the numbers from one to seventeen. Some commentators have attempted to find some theological association for each number from one to seventeen but their imaginative efforts stretched credulity beyond acceptable limits.

An interpretation that appeals to me makes a pyramid or triangle of the numbers from one to seventeen. Put one dot at the top, two on the next line, three, four and so on until there are seventeen on the base line. What is so special about seventeen? This is where the connection with Chapter 6 through the use of the name Tiberias for the sea is important. It was there that the five loaves were used to feed the vast crowd and there were twelve baskets left over. Add five to twelve for seventeen. It makes the point that at the heart of the universal mission of the church is the sustenance of Jesus as the Bread of Life.

Connecting

The link between this meal on the shore and the great discourse on the Bread of Life in Chapter Six invites us to reflect on our encounter with the risen Lord in the celebration of the Eucharist.

People who ordinarily are involved in providing for life, like the seven men gone fishing, leave their occupations to gather in the name of the Lord. As the apostles took direction from the word of the Lord on the shore, those who participate in the Eucharist first listen to his word which sustains their faith.

When our experience on the sea of life has been of empty nets, failure and darkness, then more than ever we must be alert for a direction from the word of the Lord.

Recalling that the Lord asked the apostles to offer some of the fruit of their labours, we bring forward bread and wine to represent the fruit of the earth and the work of human hands. Jesus, who identified himself as the Bread of Life who had come down from heaven, provided bread for breakfast on the shore that Easter morning. And in the Eucharist he provides the sacred bread of his divine presence to be consumed that he might strengthen us. In the traditional saying, we become what we receive. Those who receive in faith receive an infusion of divine energy to fit them for Christian mission. Communion literally means a shared responsibility or mission. Then at the end of the celebration those who have heard the word of the Lord and who have been fed on the bread of his presence are sent out to love and serve the Lord. In deep faith and gratitude they respond, 'Thanks be to God.'

Where is the risen Lord encountered?
 – In listening to his word;
 – in offering our labours through the symbolic gifts of bread and wine;
 – in partaking of the sacred meal prepared by the Lord;
 – in going forth to love and serve the Lord, as we gather the broken fragments on the hillsides of life.

Praying

O Lord, we can relate to the empty nets, the aching muscles, the tiredness of frustrating work, the disappointments of labouring in the dark. We can sense the rising anxiety of having no food for the morrow.

You stand on the shore, unrecognised, a stranger in our midst. Even when you speak your voice is not recognised.

Lord, may the memory of this story strengthen our faith to see that you are always present, even though hidden in the morning mist.

May your word be heard by us, taken to heart and translated into action.

May we ever rejoice to accept your invitation to the sacred meal that you provide for us.

May we have that thrill of excitement in recognising your presence: It is the Lord!

Peter, the new Shepherd

[15]After they had finished breakfast, Jesus said to Simon Peter, 'Simon, son of John, do you love me?' And Peter answered, 'Yes, Lord, you know that I love you.' And Jesus said, 'Feed my Lambs.' [16]A second time Jesus said to him, 'Simon, son of John, do you love me?' And Peter answered, 'Yes, Lord, you know that I love you.' Jesus said to him, 'Look after my sheep.' [17]And a third time he said to him, 'Simon, son of John, do you love me?'

Peter was saddened because Jesus asked him a third time, 'Do you love me?' and he said, 'Lord, you know everything; you know that I love you.'

Jesus then said, 'Feed my sheep. [18]Truly, I say to you, when you were young you put on your belt and walked where you liked. But when you grow old, you will stretch out your hands and another will put a belt around you and lead you where you do not wish to go.' [19]Jesus spoke like this to show the kind of death by which Peter was to glorify God. And he added, 'Follow me.'

[20]Peter looked back and saw that the disciple Jesus loved, was following as well, the one who had reclined close to Jesus at the supper and had asked him, 'Lord, who is to betray you?' [21]On seeing him Peter asked Jesus, 'Lord, what about him?' [22]Jesus answered, 'If I want him to remain until I come, does that concern you? Follow me.' [23]Because of this the rumor spread among the brothers that this disciple would not die. Yet Jesus had not said to Peter, 'He will not die', but 'suppose I want him to remain until I come.'

The charcoal fire on the shore (21:9) is a link with that other charcoal fire (18:18) where Peter had three times denied any association with Jesus. The old name, Simon, is joined to the new name, Peter, as the evangelist links his sinful past with his graced future.

After the meal, when strength is restored, Jesus addressed him, 'Simon, son of John.' Peter must have felt uncomfortable as it was usually bad news when the Lord used his old name. Like that night when Jesus warned him how much Satan would try to sift them all like wheat (Lk 22:31). Now it is a reminder of his three denials. But as in the case of Thomas who had to touch his own inner wounds, here the purpose of the Lord is to bring Simon Peter back to that great love in his heart which was obscured for a while by feelings of guilt.

'Do you love me more than these?' The question can be understood in two senses. 'Do you love me more than you love these nets and boats?' Or else, 'Is your love for me greater than that of the others here?' Whichever sense is intended, the answer of Peter is an unequivocal 'Yes!'

The evangelist, writing in Greek, uses two different verbs for what is translated as love. In the first and second questionings Jesus asks *'agapas* me' ... the holy, unselfish sort of love. But on the third occasion Jesus asks *'phileis* me'. This refers to the more common, human sort of love between good friends. And this upsets Peter. It probes more deeply under what might be a pious cover. Do you like me? Are you comfortable with me? It can be easy enough to give the pious answer that we love God. But are we comfortable with God? Do we spend time with God as with a great friend?

The probing question moves Peter to cast away every mask and reveal his inner heart. 'Lord, you know everything; you know that I love you.' It may have been an upsetting process but the Lord used it to help Peter to recognise all the love that was deep in his heart, though for a time it may have been hidden by his feelings of guilt. On the basis of his rediscovered love he is totally rehabilitated and the Lord, the Good Shepherd, now appoints him to the pastoral role of feeding and caring for the flock, young and old. It must never be forgotten that love was the one quality that the Lord looked for before he bestowed this position of authority. Authority among Christ's followers should never be seen as anything other than loving service.

There is great flexibility in the world of imagery. Jesus was the Shepherd who became the Paschal Lamb. Peter was a fisherman who became a shepherd and would later be called to follow the path of the Good Shepherd in laying down his life in a death which gave glory to God. On the human level his maturing would be complete. Once impetuous and headstrong, he would be led meekly like a lamb to the slaughter.

Connecting

The blessedness of Peter in the gospels is unique. He alone is given that name which means a rock on which Jesus would build his church (Mt 16:18). He alone received that special prayer of Jesus for the strength to recover to enable him to support the others in turn (Lk 22:32). And now, he alone is personally appointed by the Good Shepherd to feed and look after his flock.

Visiting the Holy Land, it was at Tabgha, the reputed site of this lakeside encounter, more than any other place that I felt very close to the event.

In bronze statuary the tall figure of Christ stretches out his right hand to overshadow the kneeling Peter, arched back to look beseechingly into the face of the Lord. The left hand of Jesus holds the shepherd's staff which he is about to give to Peter.

The place touched me very deeply because of the great consolation that the memory of Peter inspires. Peter was an earthly man with obvious faults and regrettable failures, yet he was called by Jesus and was given the name Peter to indicate his vocation as the rock of the church. He was severely sifted like wheat from chaff by Satan, but by the prayer of Jesus he recovered to strengthen the others. Although he, three times, denied all association with Jesus, yet his love remained deep in his heart. He was rehabilitated and appointed shepherd of the flock.

Peter is an icon of the church, human to a fault but divine by appointment. I can feel at home in this church associated with Peter. At home with my earthly failings: yet inspired by the memory of what the grace of God can do. The example of Peter encourages me too to take up the invitation of Jesus, 'Follow me.'

Praying

O Lord, you search me and you know me. You probe the innermost secrets of the heart. All my ways lie open to you. You know who I am underneath all my masks and poses.

May we respond to your gentle probing. May we have the courage to be honest with ourselves. May we find a solid rock of love at the foundation of our lives. May we build everything in life on this foundation of love.

May your Holy Spirit develop the fruits of Christian life in us, enabling us to reach out to others with your love.

In the little acre of life that we tend, may we too feed your lambs and look after your sheep.

Signs of Faith

20 [30]There were many other signs that Jesus gave in the presence of his disciples but they are not recorded in this book. [31]These are recorded so that you may believe that Jesus is the Christ, the Son of God; believe and you will have life through his Name.

21 [24]It is this disciple who testifies about the things he has recorded here and we know that his testimony is true. [25]But Jesus did many other things; if all were written down, the world itself would not hold the books recording them.

There are two conclusions to this gospel, the original ending at the close of Chapter 20 and then the last verses of the Chapter 21 which was added later. The writer of the latter ending vouches for the authenticity of all that has been written. And he adds a nice, human touch about the inability of any book to capture the total story of Jesus.

The conclusion to Chapter 20 also makes the point that we are being given only a selection of all that Jesus did. The evangelist tells the reader that his purpose was to select those actions of Jesus which had a sign value. A sign is something that points beyond itself to a greater reality. We see a road sign, take direction and move on towards our destination. John wants the reader to move on from the action of Jesus to belief in his divinity. The miracles recounted by him point to Jesus as the Christ, the Son of God. But belief is a free act and the reaction to the various signs showed that there were many who refused to believe. They remained in the dark. But those who moved forward into faith were given life, eternal life, a sharing in divine life as children of God.

Seven Signs

John counts the miracle at the Cana wedding as the first sign

given by Jesus, and the healing of the official's son as the second. He does not number the other miraculous acts, but given his interest in numbers, it comes as no surprise to recognise seven signs, each of which is a story developed at some depth.
1. Water changed into wine (2:1-12).
2. Cure of the official's son (4:46-54).
3. Healing of the crippled man (5:1-47).
4. Multiplication of loaves and fishes followed by crossing the sea (6:1-71).
5. Healing of the blind man (9:1-41).
6. Resuscitation of Lazarus (11:1-41).
7. The flow of blood and water from the side of Jesus (19: 25-28).

In the fourth sign, there is no development of the miraculous crossing of the sea as this is included with the feeding of the multitude as two parts of the one passover sign. Set in the context of the Feast of Passover, these reminders of the Exodus are developed in the long discourse on the bread of life.

The seven signs are to be arranged in a chiastic or criss-cross design which reveals remarkable similarity between the connected events.

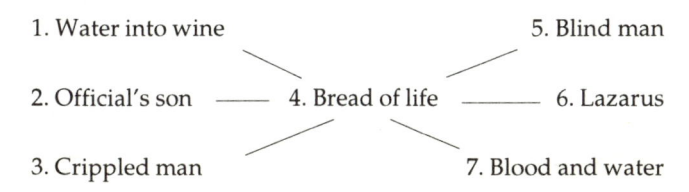

1. Water into wine   5. Blind man

2. Official's son   ——   4. Bread of life   ——   6. Lazarus

3. Crippled man   7. Blood and water

The first sign connects with the seventh: the second with the sixth: the third with the fifth. All the connecting lines pass through the fourth. In this chiastic construction focus is directed towards the importance of the central event, the fourth.

The first sign is about water and wine while the seventh is about blood and water. The wedding of heaven and earth was foretold in the sign at Cana and it was effected in the going of Jesus to the Father on Calvary. It is the new Passover, celebrated by the followers of Jesus in the water of baptism and the blood of the Eucharist.

The healing of the official's son has several parallels with the raising of Lazarus. At the beginning of each story, word is brought to Jesus about somebody at the point of death. Each miracle occurred after two days and after a journey between Judea and Galilee. In both cases the participants are questioned about their belief. The official is told that his son will live and Martha is told that her brother will rise again. After each miracle we are told that many came to believe in Jesus. These two signs point to the power over death which Jesus had. He came to bring eternal life to all who believe in him.

The healing of the cripple at the pool is closely connected with the cure of the blind man. Both miracles are done at a pool in Jerusalem on the Sabbath. The two men who were healed were interrogated at length by the Jews. In each case the controversy is about the attitude of Jesus to the Sabbath observance and what this is saying about his relationship with the Father. At the end of these two episodes we are told of the unbelief of the Jews. Christians see the pool of healing water as a symbol of baptism which releases from the paralysis of sin and leads to a life of light.

All three connecting lines pass through the fourth sign, the double reminder of the first Passover and the exodus. Jesus develops the significance of the miracle of the bread in his discourse on the bread of life. He is the bread come down from heaven in the wisdom of his teaching which he had given and in the bread of his flesh to eat which he would give for the time after his ascension.

In this criss-cross construction the central episode is the dynamic source and summit of all the others. Christians appreciate this Johannine insight in calling the Eucharist, with its tables of the word and of the sacred bread, the summit and the source of Christian life.

Incidentally, if the seven petitions of the Our Father were to be set out in a similar chiastic design, the fourth and central petition is 'Give us today our daily bread.' Our common translation as daily is totally inadequate. The original word in the Greek of the gospels of Matthew and Luke refers to a bread beyond substantial matter. Only Christ is the Bread in this sense. Again the structure of the prayer points to the Eucharist as the central celebration and source of Christian life.

Mary at Cana and Calvary

The mother of Jesus appears in two places in John's gospel, at the wedding in Cana and on Calvary. There are very deliberate parallels between the two episodes.

- At Cana, the first sign of divine glory was given by Jesus when he changed water into wine. On Calvary, the last sign was the flowing of water and blood from his side.
- Each sign is linked with faith. After seeing the sign at Cana the disciples believed. The sign on Calvary gets personal authentication from the evangelist so that the reader too might believe.
- At Cana, Jesus said that his hour had not yet come. The hour of Jesus refers to the events of his passing to the Father.
- Obedience is prominent in each place. Mary told the servants to do whatever Jesus told them. On Calvary, Jesus obediently fulfilled the scriptures until he can finally say, 'It is accomplished.'
- In neither place is the name of Mary mentioned but she is introduced as the mother of Jesus. In each place she is addressed by Jesus as Woman, a title also addressed to the Samaritan woman and to Mary of Magdala. It sounds cold in English translation but in the spoken language of that time it was a noble title. It may have been used to evoke the reference in Genesis 3:15 to the woman whose offspring would crush the head of the serpent.

Had Jesus addressed Mary as *mother* he would have referred to their flesh and blood relationship in family. But by calling her *woman* he opened up a wider sense of motherhood in God's plan for her.

Her wider motherhood emerges at Cana. She showed a maternal solicitude for the family who were facing the embarrassment of running out of wine. In bringing their need to Jesus she interceded on their behalf. To intercede literally means to stand between parties.

She interceded as only a mother might. Jesus said that his hour had not yet come. But we can see how she disregarded his hesitation in a way that only a mother might. Totally confident that her Son would accede to her request, she told the servants, 'Do whatever he tells you.' Mary's influence on one's life will always be towards the will of her Blessed Son.

So, at Cana Mary showed a maternal solicitude for the needs of people. She interceded on their behalf with the confidence of a mother and she directed the people to do his will.

The evangelist connects this first miraculous sign of divine glory with the faith of the first disciples. 'In this way he let his Glory appear and his disciples believed in him.' Their faith is a response to the sign.

What about Mary? When did she believe? Her approach to her Son shows that she believed before the miracle was performed. There is an old principle in theology that what God wants to effect in many people he first accomplishes in one. In other words, God writes a headline in one person for others to copy. This headline person is a chosen model.

In the Old Testament the model of faith is Abraham. Because of his fidelity he became the father of many believers in the centuries after him. In the New Testament the first person to show faith in Jesus was Mary, whose faith was associated with that first sign of divine glory which brought faith to the disciples. She was the first cell in the body of believers, namely the church. Having seen the sign the disciples believed. The one cell had become many. The number of disciples multiplied rapidly and today numbers hundreds of millions. Hence, Mary, the first cell of faith, can be called the Mother of the Church for a mother is a cell of life which is multiplied as she gives life to another.

Her wider motherhood was confirmed on Calvary. According

to John, the last words addressed by Jesus to any disciple were to the beloved disciple: 'Behold your mother.' The word *behold* occurs nineteen times in John, usually introducing a moment of revelation ... Behold the Lamb of God ... Behold the man ... Behold your king.

We notice that Jesus did not say 'Behold my mother' but 'your mother'. The beloved disciples who is not named is someone who represents all who believe in the Lord and love him. 'He made a place for her in his home'. On the individual level it means that he provided a home for her. And on the representative level he stands for all who take her into their hearts and devotion as mother.

A mother's role does not cease at giving birth. It grows into a very special relationship of loving and caring. The care of Mary for the infant church is seen in her prayerful presence, specially noted by Luke, in the upper room as the apostles awaited the promised Spirit (Acts 1:14).

Mary is recognised as the model of believers and the mother of the Church.

Behold your mother!

Behold, come and see what great things God has done in her.

Ponder all these things in your heart.

Come and understand the heights of grace to which the Church is called.

Look on her as Mother, the first living cell of faith and whose maternal love continues to care for all her children.

Come, behold her relationship with you and take her to the home of your heart.